THE STRUCTURE OF MUSIC

THE
STRUCTURE OF
MUSIC

An Outline for Students

R. O. MORRIS

London
OXFORD UNIVERSITY PRESS

Oxford University Press, Ely House, London W. 1

LONDON OXFORD GLASGOW NEW YORK
TORONTO MELBOURNE WELLINGTON CAPE TOWN
IBADAN NAIROBI DAR ES SALAAM LUSAKA ADDIS ABABA
KUALA LUMPUR SINGAPORE JAKARTA HONG KONG TOKYO
DELHI BOMBAY CALCUTTA MADRAS KARACHI

ISBN 0 19 317310 7

First edition 1935
Thirteenth impression 1976

Printed in Great Britain
at the University Press, Oxford
by Vivian Ridler
Printer to the University

Foreword

I am greatly indebted to my colleague, Mr. S. P. Waddington, for his kindness in reading the whole of the text beforehand; many amendments and modifications of detail are due to his careful revision. Valuable suggestions were also made by Dr. Vaughan Williams and Professor Buck; nor can I forbear to acknowledge the stimulus and encouragement received in the preliminary stages from the late Gustav Holst. The subject appealed strongly to him, and right up to within two or three days of his fatal operation he was discussing, with the greatest zest and enthusiasm, what the scope and content of the book ought to be.

R. O. M.

CHELSEA
Nov. 1934

Introduction

This little book is of the nature of a compendium, and is compiled purely for the convenience of students. There is probably not one of the forms here discussed which is not fully described and illustrated, under the appropriate heading, in *Grove's Dictionary*, the *Encyclopaedia Britannica*, or similar works. But the *Encyclopaedia* is not always available just when and where one wants it, and even the indispensable Grove costs—for a student—a good deal of money and can hardly be stowed away in a suitcase. It will therefore be a convenience to many to have the necessary information collected in a portable and inexpensive form; and that is all that this volume attempts to do.

Form in the musical sense is not easily defined; in some contexts it may mean a good deal more or less than in others. Ideally speaking, it is felt to be something vital and growing, an organism, rather than a mould or framework. Consider any of the really great specimens of musical architecture—such things as the C sharp minor Fugue in Book I of the 'Forty-Eight'; the Prelude to 'Tristan'; the first movement of the 'Eroica' Symphony.

One could take any of these as a model, and copy it, bar by bar, cadence by cadence, modulation by modulation; but would anyone say of the result, 'Of course the ideas are third-rate, but as a specimen of form your work is truly superb'? He would not, and he would be right; we feel instinctively and without question that he would be right.

What this implies, of course, is that in the last analysis form and content cannot be wholly independent of one another, or even exist at all apart from one another. When we think of the 'Tristan' Prelude as an ideally satisfying example of musical form, we are thinking, consciously or otherwise, of all the elements that go to build it up—the harmonies, the rhythms, the dynamics. In this sense the form is conditioned by the content;

the form of every genuine piece of music is therefore unique. It is not a subject for analysis, but for direct experience—those 'adventures of the soul among masterpieces' whose description, so far as they can be described, is a task for the critic, not for the analyst. In these pages 'form' will be taken in its more obvious and limited sense; our task will be, not to find out wherein one piece of music differs from another, but what, structurally speaking, they have in common. We shall deal, not with the living growth, but with the bony framework; we shall not seek to define what makes any piece of music great or unique, but what makes it organically intelligible—a comparatively humble task, it may be, yet not lacking an interest of its own, and not safely to be neglected by students of music.

In this connexion we have first of all to distinguish names that imply a certain type of structure or a certain grouping of movements—e.g. rondo, suite—from those which have merely a vague association with the style or content of the musical thought—e.g. rhapsody, impromptu, nocturne. Take such a familiar term as 'prelude'; surely a reader of this book may hope, by the time he has finished it, to know what a prelude is? Yet a moment's thought will show that this is impossible. Consider only Bach's 'Forty-Eight', and from these select, say, those in C major, E♭ major, A major and B♭ major, in Book I, and those in C♯ minor, D major, and F minor, in Book II. What, structurally, have these in common with one another? What is the common factor of 'L'Après-midi d'un Faune' and the 'Tristan' Prelude? So also with other varieties of nomenclature; can one collate Purcell's Fantasias for Strings in 3, 4, and 5 parts with Bach's 'Fantasia Cromatica', or Vaughan Williams's 'Fantasia on a Theme by Thomas Tallis'? How parallel one of Liszt's Hungarian Rhapsodies with Delius's *Brigg Fair* (which is a free set of variations) or with Brahms's Rhapsody in G minor, op. 79 (which is in the strictest first-movement form)?

Such questions answer themselves, and it will be found that the number of genuine structural archetypes in music is not very large. None the less they have to be sorted out into some kind of order, for the sake of clearness. On the whole, it seemed that the traditional classification into 'harmonic' and 'contrapuntal' forms would serve as well as another. It involves a cross-division, of course, for many 'harmonic' movements contain purely 'contrapuntal' passages, and 'harmonic' assemblages like the Suite and the Sonata often contain one or even more movements—canzona, canon, or fugue—that belong definitely to the 'contrapuntal' family. Moreover, the terms themselves relate primarily to texture rather than to design. But though the classification is thus an arbitrary one, it works fairly well, and there is no more obviously satisfactory one to take its place. So there it is.

It is clearly out of the question in a work of this kind to quote whole movements in illustration of the various methods of design. To do so would swell the bulk of the volume to a prodigious extent and add enormously to the cost—precisely the two things above all others which it is most desired to avoid. Necessity has therefore been made into a virtue, and the illustrations given mainly by reference and not by direct quotation. Every effort has been made to take these illustrations from universally accessible and familiar works, such as the Bach suites and partitas, the 'Forty-Eight', the pianoforte sonatas of Mozart and Beethoven, the best-known classical concertos. Anyone possessing these will be able to follow almost every step in the argument; anyone not possessing them, or not able, by fair means or foul, to become possessed of them, will find this work of no interest or benefit. This is no idle warning, for many students are strangely unalive to the absolute necessity of forming a small working library of their own. They do not seem to realize that such a nucleus forms an essential part of a musician's working capital, and that such works as those mentioned above must be included in its minimum requirements. So let it be repeated: unless these works are close to hand for immediate and continuous reference, it is pure waste of time to read this book.

Contents

INTRODUCTION   vii

PART I
THE HARMONIC FORMS

I. ELEMENTARY PRINCIPLES OF MELODIC FORM   3

II. HOW PERIODS AND SECTIONS ARE BUILT UP   9

III. THE SUITE   16

IV. THE SONATA, AS A WHOLE   27

V. FIRST-MOVEMENT FORM   39

VI. RONDO FORM   58

VII. THE CONCERTO   63

VIII. VARIATION FORM. THE OVERTURE   74

PART II
THE CONTRAPUNTAL FORMS

IX. THE ANTECEDENTS OF FUGUE   87

X. FUGUE   95

XI. SPECIAL TYPES OF FUGUE. CANON, ROUND,
AND CATCH. CHORALE PRELUDES   110

APPENDIX. ON VOCAL FORMS, AND THE
SYMPHONIC POEM   125

INDEXES   129

PART I

THE HARMONIC FORMS

I

Elementary Principles of Melodic Form

The earliest forms of secular music were closely associated with the song and the dance; they depend, that is to say, on the length and metre of the poetic stanza, or on the prescribed movements of the dancers. The direct influence of the dance on later music will be more conveniently discussed in relation to the suite (Ch. III); in this chapter it is the organization of simple melodies, directly connected with folk-poetry and ballad-poetry, that is to be considered.

Four principles suggest themselves immediately as capable of imparting order and shapeliness to a series of musical notes:

A. Unity of time.
B. Unity of key.
C. Balance of phrase.
D. The employment of a pattern unit, either by repetition or by sequence.

A. *Unity of Time*

This scarcely needs illustrating. This may seem questionable to those who have heard tell of the varied times and rhythmic freedom of the folk-song; but it is a fact nevertheless that the old tune-writers—those mysterious anonymities—preferred to keep to a regular time, and generally did so unless there was some abrupt change or irregularity in the metre of the words that made it impossible. Curiosity on this point led me to pick up—quite at random—the first volume of Cecil Sharp's *Folk Songs from Somerset* (the original edition), and a search through the twenty-seven songs gives the following results:

1–6. All quite regular.

7 (*Cold blows the Wind*). Regular in its irregularity, the ten bars being made up as follows:

6 9 6 6   6 9 6 6   6 6
8 8 8 8   8 8 8 8   8 8,

the last two bars being merely a reiteration, both words and music, of the two preceding.

8–21. All quite regular.

22 (*Barbara Ellen*). Regular $\frac{5}{4}$ time throughout except for a single bar (the fourth) of common time. This irregularity is undoubtedly due to the singer rather than to the composer. As Sharp himself points out (*English Folk Song; Some Conclusions,* p. 79), 'a phrase is sometimes curtailed owing to the disinclination to wait the prescribed number of beats on the last note'. This is especially common, one might add, in $\frac{5}{4}$ tunes such as this.

23. 8 bars of regular common time, then a change to $\frac{6}{4}$ time, which is kept for the three remaining bars of the tune.

24. Regular.

25. Regular common time, except for two bars of $\frac{3}{4}$ time inserted to meet the requirements of the penultimate line of the metrical stanza, which is shorter than the rest.

26, 27. Regular.

From this tabulation one may fairly conclude that unity of time was early recognized as an essential feature in the artistic organization of melody.

B. *Unity of Key*

In dealing with folk-song melodies of the type just reviewed one should speak of mode rather than of key, for many of them date back to a time when the transition from the modal to the diatonic system had not yet been made. Modulation in our sense of the word, therefore, is not to be looked for; unity is obtained by adhering throughout to the notes proper to the mode, and by employing the more important notes of the mode, like the first and fifth—tonic and dominant, as we should say nowadays—at the nodal points, especially at the beginning and at the final cadence. When the actual opening notes are neither tonic nor dominant there is a strong tendency to close the opening phrase on the tonic, so as to declare the mode without undue delay. Take for example the opening phrases of *The Sweet Primèroses*:

and *Cold blows the Wind*:

Both of these start on the mediant and proceed immediately to the next above it; the rest of the phrase is accordingly shaped so as to leave no doubt in the listener's mind that G in the first case and D in the second is the final of the mode, or, as we should now say, the key-note. The last phrase ends in every case on the key-note; in harmonized music, such a precaution of course is unnecessary, for any note of the tonic chord will serve; but when melody had only its own resources to rely on, it preferred to leave nothing to chance, and to close definitely and unmistakably on the actual key-note.

In popular songs of a later period, when the old modes had given place to our major and minor scales, the device of modulation is freely employed—so much so that one really need not give examples; such tunes as *Rule Britannia, The Minstrel Boy, The Blue Bell of Scotland*, will occur at once to everyone. The guiding principles are that the modulations must only take place to closely related keys, and that the supremacy of the tonic must not be endangered. The function of modulation is to supply variety, that of the tonic is to maintain unity. This principle— that of combining unity with variety—is at the root of all artistic form, from a Ming bowl to a Gothic cathedral, from the humblest folk-song up to the greatest symphony. The composers of the older folk-songs could not modulate, they had to keep to the notes of their mode—but they took good care not to end all their phrases on the same note of the mode, and in this way they achieved a variety similar in kind to that which their successors obtained by modulation.

c. *Balance of Phrase*

This will be discussed at greater length in the next chapter, where the construction of more elaborate musical sentences and paragraphs is considered in detail. In the simple song melodies we have been examining hitherto balance of phrase certainly exists, but only, so to speak, as an accident; that is to say, it is made inevitable by the balanced construction of the verse. If you look at the words of any representative group of folk-songs or popular ballads (those tabulated in § A of this chapter, for example), you will find that practically every line ends with a stop of some kind—not necessarily a full stop, of course. In setting these words to melody, the employment of cadences[1] to coincide with these metrical stopping places is adopted instinctively and as it were automatically; just as the stanza divides into lines in accordance with its own metrical scheme, so the melody divides into phrases corresponding to that scheme. Moreover, a very large proportion of the stanzas is of the common four-line type, so that a musical structure built up of four more or less equally balanced phrases is likewise of very common occurrence. It was indeed this type of four-phrase musical period which more than any other influenced the construction of later music of a purely instrumental type, as will presently appear.

Balance of phrase is commonly reinforced by the employment of some recognizable note pattern, to heighten the sense of artistic unity. The two things are quite distinct, however, and it is perfectly possible to achieve an ordered symmetry of effect without repeating any melodic or rhythmical pattern. An excellent example is *The Seeds of Love,* published as No. 1 in Sharp's collection, and one of the best known of them all:

[1] The proper definition of the term 'cadence' is discussed in the following chapter.

Sharp himself[2] gives other examples of such construction; a very well-known and much-quoted instance of the same kind, but of a totally different style and period, is the tune which opens the slow movement of Beethoven's so-called 'Sonata pathétique' (op. 13, C minor).

D. *Pattern*

More frequently, however, both in folk-tunes and in music of a more highly organized type, pattern is employed to some extent as an element of construction. The pattern may be repeated exactly, or it may be varied; it may be repeated at the same pitch or at a different pitch (as in Sequence), but its presence as a unifying element always serves the same purpose. Its function is essentially cohesive. As an example, let us look first at an extremely fine and extremely familiar tune—*High Germany*:

This tune is of a type expressed diagrammatically as a b b a, or more accurately as a b b′ a′, the dashes indicating that the pattern phrase, though clearly recognizable, is slightly varied at its repetition. This, as Sharp points out, is a common pattern; he himself quotes *The Banks of the Sweet Dundee* as an example of it. a b a c is also not uncommon; in theory any combination or permutation of a b c should be capable of giving a satisfactory result. Were this a discourse on folk-song, it would be of interest to examine a large number of the melodies in detail, with a view to finding out which of the possible combinations are actually employed, and with what degree of frequency. But so exhaustive an analysis would scarcely serve the present purpose. What is of interest, is to find that one of the commonest, perhaps actually

[2] Op. cit., p. 77.

the commonest, of all pattern-schemes is that represented by the diagram A A B A, or (in musical notation) A: ‖ B A.

This is, in its simplest form, what has come to be known in music as the 'ternary' type of structure. As it stands, it is obviously an epitome, in miniature, of the later first-movement form. Tovey points out (*Ency. Brit.*, 'Sonata Forms') that in strict logic this is not ternary at all, but binary, the two halves being made equal by the repetition of the first strain.

In practice, however, when this structure was adopted and developed for instrumental purposes, *both* halves as a rule were repeated, the form as we know it being represented by the diagram ‖: A: ‖: B A: ‖. Thus the repeats cancel out, and, in any case, it is now too late in the day to begin describing such a formation as 'binary'. When a clause of contrast is followed by a final recapitulation of the opening clause, musical tradition has agreed to describe the structure as 'ternary', and no useful purpose would be served by insisting overmuch on the strictly etymological significance of the term. I will say no more of this now, as the general classification of forms into 'binary' and 'ternary' is discussed in Chapter III (see pp. 24, 25).

I have not been able, as a matter of fact, to find a single specimen of an A B A (as distinct from A: ‖ B A) tune in English folk-song or popular song. To repeat what has already been said, the form of the tune depends on the form of the verbal stanza, and these, in the great majority of cases, are of the four- and eight-line type. Six-line stanzas exist, of course, but in no case that I know of are the last two lines set to the same melodic phrases as the first two. Hadow quotes[3] two three-line specimens from Hungarian and Galician folk-song; but the best examples of this structure are not to be found in folk-music at all, but in such themes as Elgar's 'Enigma', or that of Schumann on which Brahms wrote his early set of pianoforte variations (op. 9).

---

[3] *Sonata Form*, p. 29.

II

How Periods and Sections are Built Up

Our task in this chapter is to observe the application of the fore-going principles—those illustrated in Chapter I—to music of a somewhat more complex type, though still of a definitely melodic and lyrical character. Before starting the analysis it will be con-venient to define certain terms in general use. Some or all of these terms have already been employed in this book, but as their full definition has to be made to some extent in terms of harmony, it seemed best to defer it until this chapter, as we have hitherto been concerned with music of a purely melodic type.

1. *The Unit (or Figure)*

This may be defined as the smallest possible component of a musical phrase. To be a recognizable entity at all, it must have rhythm, and hence cannot conceivably consist of less than two notes; almost invariably it will be found to consist of not less than three or four. Thus the first four notes of Beethoven's Fifth Symphony,

and the first six notes of his Eighth,

are vitally important units—germs, as it were, from which whole sections are eventually developed.

2. *The Phrase*

This term is extremely difficult to define with precision. The *S.O.E.D.* calls it 'Any short passage forming a more or less independent member of a longer passage'; but this definition might equally well apply to a sentence. Parry says (in *Grove's Dictionary*): 'The word is not and cannot be used with much exactness and uniformity.' I think we shall get the clearest impression of it by comparing it to a clause in speech or writing—i.e. something that comes to a stop (and is to that extent self-subsistent) and yet cannot stand by itself; complete in one sense, it is incomplete in another. As we shall be examining the slow movement of Beethoven's Sonata in F minor (op. 2, No. 1) later, take the first three and a half bars of that as an example, if one is needed.

3. *The Sentence or Period*

This is a complex of two or more phrases, complete in itself, and frequently marked, in classical usage, by a perfect cadence. It may or may not exhibit unity of key—that will depend on its relation to the whole section of which it forms a part. In the movement just quoted, for instance (from Beethoven's op. 2, No. 1), the opening sentence is one of eight bars, rounded by a full close in the tonic key; in the corresponding movement of his op. 28, the first sentence ends with a modulation to the dominant.

4. *Cadence*

This is another term whose definition is not easy. We all know what a cadence is, but to define it except in terms of itself is another matter. Anyone who has taught these subjects will know that the following conversation piece is no caricature of what actually happens:

Q. What is a perfect cadence?
A. The tonic chord, preceded by the dominant, constitutes a perfect cadence.
Q. Invariably?
A. No; only when they come in a cadential place.

The *S.O.E.D.* says: 'The close of a musical movement or phrase'; Parry (in *Grove's Dictionary*): 'Cadences, or (as they are often called) Closes, are the devices which in music answer the purpose of stops in language.' Both these are good, the latter being the more illuminating of the two. If anyone complains that 'devices' is too vague a word to be quite satisfactory in a definition of this kind, I invite him to suggest—or devise—a better one.

Of course the four familiar types of cadence—the perfect, the imperfect, the plagal, the interrupted—are those almost invariably employed in classical music; but the definitions given above make it clear that cadence does not *necessarily* involve harmony at all, and also that quite other harmonic progressions than the four enumerated above might be made to serve a cadential purpose. It must be admitted at the same time that ultra-modern music, while deliberately eschewing the use of classical cadence, has not been very successful in finding a substitute for it.

So far as terminology goes, the ground is now more or less clear, and the rest of the chapter can be devoted to the analysis of some representative passages. Only small-scale analysis—the analysis of sections into their component phrases and sentences —will be undertaken here; the broader analysis of movements as a whole into their principal subdivisions will be left for later chapters.

Turn first to the opening section (bars 1 to 16) of the slow movement of Beethoven's Sonata in F minor (op. 2, No. 1), to which reference has already been made.

Total length, 16 bars. It starts with an anacrusis (or upbeat) on the third beat, and ends with a perfect cadence of the 'feminine' type, in the tonic key (F major) on the second beat. There are therefore no odd beats to be accounted for. The analysis (a very simple and straightforward one) is as follows:

(1) Bars 1–8. First sentence, divisible into two four-bar phrases, the first of which ends with a half close, the second with a full close, all in the tonic, with no modulation. Note that the opening unit recurs at the opening of the second phrase; also that this phrase is an unbroken one of four bars, whilst the first one is clearly divisible into two sub-phrases of equal length, each of them rounded with a half close.

(2) Bars 9–12. A contrasting sentence of four bars, also with an

upbeat and a 'feminine' cadence, this time in C major, the dominant pedal with which the sentence opens being held on until it ultimately becomes the tonic.

(3) Bars 13–16. Concluding sentence, also of four bars, re-asserting the tonic key, starting again with the opening unit (in the higher octave), but concluding with an entirely new phrase.

The whole thus consists of four four-bar groups, in which the A A' B A" pattern is clearly recognizable.

Without carrying on the analysis in detail, let us also look at the next section (bar 17, or, to be more precise, the last beat of bar 16, to the first beat of bar 32), for it illustrates two or three points of interest—points, too, of a kind one is continually meeting.

First of all, note the overlap at the junction of bars 22 and 23. The third phrase of the sentence starting at bar 17 is a three-bar one:

but the last two notes also belong to the next phrase, as the repetition of them in bar 24 clearly shows.

Note also that this sentence—the one starting at bar 23—does not finish till the first beat of bar 27, and is therefore what is usually known as a five-bar sentence; the extra bar in this case is formed by the device of repeating the opening bar (for bar 24 is virtually a repetition of bar 23), and its object no doubt is to make good the bar shortage caused by the previous phrase being only a three-bar one. This is really being needlessly scrupulous—Beethoven in his later days would certainly not have bothered about that extra bar, any more than Haydn would.

Notice also the words above, 'what is usually known as a five-bar sentence'. By this is meant only that the sentence is pro-longed into the fifth bar. Actually it is a sentence of thirteen beats only, for only the first quaver of bar 28 belongs to it; the rest of the bar is part of the phrase that follows. There is no harm in this nomenclature provided everyone understands just what is meant by it; but to be strictly accurate one should always measure one's phrases and sentences in beats rather than in bars. If one did so, one would realize that even a so-called four-bar structure, such as prevails in this movement, is not quite so monotonously four-square as might be supposed.

Notice, finally, the further overlap at the juncture of bars 31 and 32. Most of bar 32 is of the nature of a link leading back to the recapitulation that starts with bar 32; but the repetition of the note pattern introduced in bars 28 and 30 shows that it 'looks before and after'; though it functions as a link, it is also the finish of the complete five-bar sentence which starts with the second quaver of bar 28 and finishes with the chord of F major on the first beat of bar 32.

For an example of more systematic five-bar structure in Beethoven, turn to the slow movement of the E♭ Sonata, op. 7, and look at the second half of the middle section (the movement as a whole is in extended ternary form, with coda), i.e. bars 33–51. The analysis of this is as follows:

(1) 33–7. Five-bar phrase starting in D♭, and finishing with an implied half close in C minor (the first G in bar 37 represents the resolution of the preceding chord of the augmented sixth, as well as the start of the next phrase, so that there is here another overlap).

(2) 37–41. Contrasting phrase, also of five bars (obviously in this case 2+2+1), ending with the dominant chord of B♭.

(3) 42–6. Five-bar phrase (2+1+2) founded on the opening melody; note the way in which the whole phrase is developed from the second unit.

(4) 47–51. Closely attached to the previous phrase; five bars of the 'link' type, starting on the leading seventh of C minor, and ultimately closing with a cadence in C major, the final chord of which is also the start of the recapitulation—another overlap.

The two overlaps, of course, explain how it is that a period of eighteen bars may consist of four so-called five-bar phrases.

Also of great interest, both in regard to rhythmical structure and to pattern, is the opening section of the slow movement of the D major Sonata, op. 28. This is a section of the authentic

A: ‖ : B A type, both halves being repeated; furthermore the opening sentence is formed of two decidedly similar phrases of four bars each, which might be represented as a + a′.

It is, however, the second part (bars 9–22) that is structurally most worth examining. The analysis is as follows:

(1) 9–15. Seven-bar phrase—it is hardly a sentence—on a dominant pedal, formed by the successive reiteration, first of a phrase, then of the second bar of that phrase, then of the last unit of that bar.

(2) 15–17. Link of three bars, consisting of the single un-harmonized phrase

(3) 17–22. Six-bar sentence (4 + 2), in which the opening melody is given quite a new shape by developing the unit

and adding two bars only, instead of the four that might have been expected, to form the final cadence. Once more, of course, it is the overlaps that enable one to add up 7, 3, and 6, and make the result 14.

A little analysis of this detailed sort is instructive; too much of it speedily becomes wearisome. But before passing on to the next chapter, I would ask the reader to look at the 'Largo e Mesto' of the D major Sonata, op. 10, No. 3. The opening section of this illustrates the truth of what was said above (p. 12), that for strict accuracy, phrases and sentences should be measured in beats rather than bars. Bar measurement has worked reasonably well in the analysis that has so far been carried out, but in this movement the phrases are of variable formation and cross the bar-lines quite irregularly, so that analysis by bar could only give a rough-and-ready result. There is no doubt that the section divides into four principal sub-sections, the second of which begins somewhere in bar 9, the third somewhere in bar 17, and the fourth somewhere in bar 26. But to obtain an adequate analysis of the rhythmical structure, one should certainly regard this section as consisting primarily, not of 29 bars in $\frac{6}{8}$ time, but of 174 quaver beats.

The skeleton analysis (leaving out all details of pattern, &c.) would then be as follows:

(1) Opening sub-section of 51 beats, consisting of two phrases of 25 and 21 beats respectively, with a link of 5 beats (in bar 5) between them. D minor.

(2) Second sub-section of 47 beats, consisting of three sentences of 24, 12, and 11 beats respectively, closing in C major.

(3) Third sub-section of 55 beats, consisting of two sentences of 24 and 31 beats respectively. A minor.

(4) Final sub-section (coda), consisting of a single sentence of 21 beats, clinching A minor.

From now onwards we shall not concern ourselves, except incidentally, with detailed analysis of this kind. We shall examine construction on a wider scale—the analysis of whole movements into their principal sections, and the relations of those sections to the whole and to one another. It will be assumed that the further analysis of those sections into their small components could now be carried out independently by the student with the help of the examples given in this chapter.

III

The Suite

So far as its title went, the suite was originally a special form of
sonata, which etymologically means merely 'something to be
played' as opposed to the 'something to be sung' of the cantata.
It is not intended in these pages to trace the processes of historical
origin and growth in any detail; for that, the student must be
referred to the various histories, and in particular to Parry's
articles on 'Suite' and 'Sonata' in *Grove's Dictionary*, for these are
miracles of summarization; seldom indeed is it that a compendium so tightly packed is at the same time so lucid. But
readers may be interested to know, not merely what a suite is, but
also how the suite as one of the representative art-forms hap-
pened to come into existence just when and where it did. This will
emerge clearly if the following summary of events is recalled and
kept in mind:

(1) Up till (roughly) the year 1600, popular music was something quite apart and distinct from 'educated' or 'cultured' or
whatever-you-like-to-call-it music, which was, broadly speaking,
church music. (I do not forget the madrigal; but the madrigal,
formally considered, was an offspring of the motet. It came to
perfection, and died; it was quite without influence on later
instrumental music.)

(2) Church music was vocal music, intricately polyphonic in
texture, fluid and non-accentual in rhythm; it deliberately
eschewed, as something *per se* undesirable, the strong accents and
sharply cut phrases in which popular music, and especially
popular dance music, took delight. It was, moreover, founded on
the old modal system.

(3) Within fifty years or so of this date, however, far-reaching

changes took place. Thanks largely to the efforts of the mono-
dists, i.e. the early operatic writers, the polyphonic conception
of music as a simultaneous confluence of melodies gave way to
that of a single melodic outline supported by chords. Figured
bass came into general use, and the old modal system (virtually
discarded by the later madrigalists) was replaced by the two-
scale system—a bloodless and indeed a scarcely noticed
revolution.

(4) At the same time, musical instruments began to be im-
proved out of all recognition. The old spinets and virginals had
been a great stimulus to the composers of the later sixteenth
century, in England especially. Now the harpsichord and the
clavichord took their place, whilst in Italy craftsmen of genius
devoted themselves to the stringed instruments, so that the old
lutes, viols, and gambas were superseded by the violin and the
violoncello, which far surpassed their predecessors in range,
power of tone, and brilliancy of execution.

(5) Above all, a new spirit was in the air. Everyone felt, consciously or unconsciously, that the old modes, and the old forms
and patterns that suited them, were now worked out, and that
some sort of cross-fertilization was needed if music was to be
renewed and revitalized.

It was therefore natural at this juncture that the two streams of
church music and popular music, borne hitherto on parallel and
independent courses, should converge. From their confluence
came the earliest type of sonata, of which the suite (as it afterwards came to be called) is merely one special variety—a sonata,
that is to say, in which dance movements predominate.

In this connexion, three questions immediately present themselves:

(1) What were the various dance movements that came to be
    associated, habitually or occasionally, in suites?[1]

(2) What was the nature—the time, spirit, and peculiar char-
    acteristics—of those movements taken individually?

(3) —and this, of course, is specially relevant to the present

---

[1] Or 'Lessons' (England); 'Partitas' (Germany); 'Ordres' (France).

inquiry—What methods of internal organization and construction do they exhibit?

To take these in order:

1

There was never any fixed number of movements in a suite, nor
can any one dance form be considered as an absolutely invariable member of it. But by far the commonest are the allemande,
courante, saraband, and jig, and these—usually coming in that
order—may be considered as the nucleus of a normally constituted suite. Also very frequent are the minuet, the bourrée, and
the gavotte; a very large number of suites will be found to contain one or more of these[2] in addition to the four above mentioned. Also met with occasionally are the passepied, loure,
polonaise, and (in England) hornpipe. For the sake of completeness, let us include the rigadoon and also the older pavan
and galliard, though the latter went early out of fashion, and
should be regarded as precursors of the suite, not as actual
members of it.

Before going on to describe the characteristic features of each
dance, it seems in place here to add that the suite, as we know it,
did not always consist *exclusively* of dance movements. Bach's
French Suites do—almost; but the English Suites are all headed
by a prelude of such imposing dimensions as almost to over-
weight the other movements, while the partitas also start with a
non-dance movement, to which Bach gives a different name in
each case—Prélude, Sinfonie, Fantaisie, Ouverture, Préambule,
and Toccata. Even the allemande, we must remember, is not
strictly speaking a dance. In Handel's suites[3] we find such things
as airs and fugues interspersed with the other movements, while
in the *Ordres* of Couperin almost anything may turn up. There
was a theoretical distinction between the *Sonata di Ballo,* consisting exclusively of dance movements, and the *Sonata da Camera,*

[2] No. 6 of Bach's French Suites contains all three.

[3] His second Suite, in F, does not contain a single dance movement, and is in
every respect a perfectly regular specimen of the eighteenth-century sonata.

in which dance movements were interspersed with others of a more serious character; from what has been said above, it will be gathered that both these types were ultimately merged in the suite as we find it in the early eighteenth century.

2

The individual nature of these various dances is briefly as follows:

Allemande

Although an almost invariable member of the suite, this is not really a dance form at all. It is a quietly flowing movement, $\frac{4}{4}$ time, moderate tempo. It starts as a rule with an upbeat of a single semiquaver, or, more rarely, of three semiquavers, and the texture is often more consistently polyphonic than that employed in the rest of the suite, except the jig.

Courante

This exists in two quite distinct forms, the Italian and the French. The Italian is a lively running movement in simple triple time—usually $\frac{3}{4}$ or $\frac{3}{8}$. The French is less lively in pace, and is written, for the most part, in $\frac{3}{2}$ time, changing at the cadence— and occasionally for a bar or so in the course of the movement— to $\frac{6}{4}$. One may even find bars in which one hand plays in $\frac{3}{2}$, the other in $\frac{6}{4}$. Parry justly remarks that such effects are for the eye rather than the ear, and in any case, one would think, they are hardly appropriate to dance music (not, of course, that these suites were ever actually intended to be danced to).

The courante, like the allemande, starts with an odd quaver or group of quavers (or semiquavers, as the case may be).

Saraband

A slow and stately dance, in triple time, usually $\frac{3}{4}$ or $\frac{3}{2}$. It starts on the downbeat, and shows a strong tendency to halt periodic- ally on the second beat. So marked a characteristic is this, that where it is completely ignored—as in the so-called saraband of

Bach's French Suite in B minor—one feels that the very title of saraband is a misnomer.

A saraband may be followed by one or more 'Doubles', in which the essential material is repeated, but with a uniformly running accompaniment of crotchets (in $\frac{3}{2}$ time) or quavers (in $\frac{3}{4}$ time).

Jig

This is the least uniform of all the suite members. It comes last, it is lively, it is usually in some variety of triple or compound time, and that is about all one can safely say of it. $\frac{3}{8}$, $\frac{6}{8}$, $\frac{12}{8}$ are the commonest time-signatures, and they are the ones most easily associated with what any of us would instinctively describe as the jig type of movement. But in Bach alone one finds such varying time-signatures as ₵ (French Suite, D minor), $\frac{12}{16}$ (ditto, G major), C (Partita, B♭), $\frac{9}{16}$ (ditto, D major), ◯◯ (ditto, E minor). One should add that the jig is often treated in a definitely fugal manner, with plenty of imitation between the two hands; such a movement as the last number of the French Suite in G major might be described with perfect accuracy as a fugue in binary form, the subject being treated by inversion throughout the second half.

Minuet

At the time of which we are now writing, the minuet was essentially a courtly dance—a ceremonious affair with short steps. Time, $\frac{3}{4}$, or occasionally $\frac{3}{8}$, starting on the downbeat; tempo moderate—not more than an unhurried allegretto. Later, in Haydn's hands, and to some extent even in Mozart's, the minuet, as we shall see in Chapter IV, assumed a different character.

The minuet was frequently, though not invariably, followed by a second one (the 'Trio' of later times), usually in the same key, but occasionally in the relative or tonic major or minor. After this, there was a 'Da capo', either expressed or understood.

Bourrée

Brisk and lively, in $\frac{2}{2}$ time, starting on the fourth crotchet.

Gavotte

Sprightly in character, but less rapid than the bourrée; $\frac{4}{4}$ time, starting on the half-bar.

The gavotte was frequently followed by a second, usually of the 'musette' type, i.e. one in which a drone bass persists throughout or for the greater part of the time. After this (which borrowed its name from an old French instrument of the bagpipe family) the gavotte was repeated D.C.

Passepied

A somewhat lively dance, originally Breton, usually in $\frac{3}{8}$, but occasionally in $\frac{3}{4}$ time, and starting on the third beat.

Loure

Another dance associated (like the musette) with an instrument of the bagpipe family, from which it takes its name. $\frac{6}{4}$ time, as a rule; not by any means a slow dance, but less lively than the jig or the galliard.

Polonaise

A simple and graceful triple-time movement, whose chief peculiarity was the cadence on the second beat. It is of course very different from the grandiose conceptions of Chopin, which are rhapsodic in style and built in sections. In these, moreover, the cadence tends to come on the third rather than the second beat.

Rigaudon or Rigadoon

This was at one time very popular in England as a dance, and some consider that the French name is a corruption from the English, and not vice versa.[4] Barclay Squire, in *Grove's Dictionary*, gives some rules for its construction, and an example to illustrate them; but in purely instrumental rigadoons—e.g. Purcell's in *Musick's Handmaid*—these are ignored, and the dance becomes a straightforward binary movement, brisk in character, and in duple time.

[4] Rig, in the vernacular of those times, meant 'a saucy female'.

Hornpipe

Not to be confused with the 'Jacky Tar' variety. The true hornpipe was a triple-time dance, cadencing on the third beat of the
bar; many specimens are to be found in Purcell, both in the
suites and in the incidental dances written for stage works, such
as the *Fairy Queen*. The time as a rule is $\frac{3}{2}$. One of Purcell's—in
the Sixth Suite—is in $\frac{3}{4}$ time, but this cadences on the first beat,
and is therefore not an authentic hornpipe.

Pavan

A slow stately dance, in common time, of Italian origin, but
especially popular in the late sixteenth century in England.

Galliard

A somewhat riotous affair, in triple time, viewed with disfavour
by austere critics, but nevertheless immensely popular, and
usually linked, in music, for the sake of contrast, with the pavan
—an association that inevitably recalls the later combination of
saraband and jig. Thus Morley, in the *Plaine and Easie Introduction,* after describing the pavan as 'a kind of staide Musicke,
ordained for grave dancing', adds, 'After every Pavan we usually
set a Galliard'.

The foregoing list has been slightly extended for the sake of
completeness. Of the last seven, the pavan and galliard had disappeared from the scene before the suite as we know it came into
being, while the hornpipe is only found in the suites of Purcell,
where it takes the place of the jig. The rigadoon, for all its
popularity as a dance, does not anywhere appear, so far as my
knowledge goes, as a member of the suite, whilst the passepied,
loure, and polonaise are of rare occurrence, though specimens
of all three may be found in Bach's suites and partitas.

3

Now for a few words about the internal construction of these
dance movements. In any one suite, they are all, as a rule, in the

same key, except where there are paired movements, when the second may be in the relative or tonic major or minor; see for example Bach's English Suites, in every one of which this pairing of movements is exemplified.

The movements are for the most part in what is called 'binary' form. Of this more later; for the moment let us only remark that specimens of 'ternary' form (in the usually accepted sense), though rare, are nevertheless to be found here and there—e.g. the second minuets in the fourth of Bach's English and the third of his French Suites. There may even be a rondo (e.g. the passepied of Bach's Fifth English Suite). The other type, however, predominates, and in it the guiding principle of construction is that of key distribution, which is planned on a somewhat rigid basis. If the movement is major, the close at the double bar is made in the dominant key; if the movement is minor, the close at the double bar may be in the relative major, as in the saraband of the C minor partita; more often, however, the modulation to the major is of a transitory nature and the first part closes on the chord of the dominant. In both major and minor movements the second part is rather longer than the first, and modulation occurs more freely, though always within the select circle of 'related' keys; the return to the tonic is always made soon enough to ensure its preponderance in the general scheme of things.

This key system is not reinforced by any definite plan of thematic construction; indeed, the style of the movements is too discursive, as a rule, to have anything that could be properly called a theme. At the opening of the second part there is commonly a reference to the opening of the first part, either directly or by inversion, and the respective cadences often show a similarity in the details of their formation. Beyond that, the correspondence of the two parts is one of general style, not of phrase or figure. 'In the Suite,' says Parry (in *Grove's Dictionary*), 'the subject does not stand out at all prominently from its context, but is only a well-marked presentation of the type of motion and rhythm which is to prevail throughout the movement.' That is excellently put, and leaves nothing more to be said on that particular point.

But the distinction between 'binary' and 'ternary' still needs a somewhat fuller explanation. It lies, essentially, in the absence or presence of a recapitulation—exact or modified—of the opening period. That, as we have already seen (p. 8), is the accepted basis of it, and it is a serviceable classification, even if border-line cases do turn up now and again to set the pundits by the ears.

It was at one time judged that no movement could be considered as 'ternary' unless its opening period closed with a full cadence in the tonic key. I mention this ancient heresy for the sake of completeness, although Hadow disposed of it long ago by pointing out, in the preface to *Sonata Form,* that it involves a cross-classification in theory and produces absurd and para-doxical results in practice. One need only consider the Haydn minuets. These are all in A B A form, but in some of them the first A ends in the tonic, in others, not. Are we then to say that the latter are 'binary', but their fellows 'ternary'? Or take the ordinary fully developed first-movement form, with its three clearly marked divisions of exposition, development, and re-capitulation; do you propose to call this 'binary', simply because the close at the end of the exposition is not in the tonic? You must do so, if you start with the assumption we are considering. And if it be rejoined that such a conclusion follows logically from the given premise, one can only reply that something must be wrong with a premise that only leads to absurdities. *Alice's Adventures in Wonderland,* we may remember, is one of the most logical books ever written.

Another point that musicians have determined by general consent is that the internal structure of a movement is not affected by the repetition of the constituent sections. We may admit that on paper A B A is not quite the same thing as A A B A B A; but what about the common sense of the matter? A Haydn minuet is played with repeats before the Trio, without repeats after it, but surely no one will seriously maintain that it is in ternary form the second time but not the first? Or take two typical first movements from Beethoven's Pianoforte Sonatas, op. 81 and op. 90. In the first of these the exposition is repeated, in the second it is not; but only from sheer perversity would anyone deny that these are both perfectly normal specimens of orthodox first-movement form.

It only remains to say something about the subsequent history of the suite. By the latter part of the eighteenth century the suite, in the sense of an assemblage of dance-tunes, had disappeared, and its place was taken by the serenades, cassations, and divertimenti which we associate principally with the name of Mozart. These, however, were not composed for the keyboard, but for strings, with or without the addition of some wind instruments; they are not exactly 'chamber music' and yet not quite 'orchestral music', but a genre between the two. The names do not matter very much; 'cassation' is an obscure term of which no convincing derivation appears to have been found, while 'serenade' and 'divertimento' are self-explanatory. All are groups of pieces of no prescribed number or arrangement. They were written to please, not to edify, and the forms exhibited by their individual movements are roughly those associated with the later eighteenth-century type of sonata—first-movement form, usually with little or no development, theme and variations, rondo, and so on. All these will be fully described later on, and there is no need here to do more than mention them.

After Mozart's death the divertimento followed the suite into disuse. Beethoven, excelling in large-scale architecture, naturally preferred the more spacious forms of sonata, quartet, and symphony, whilst his romantic successors had quite other fish to fry. But towards the latter part of the nineteenth century composers began to realize that there was, after all, a place in music for groups of pieces of slighter character and less elaborate organization than the symphony. That is all that 'suite' really means nowadays. Thus understood, it is independent of any particular conventions of style, structure, and idiom, and for that reason likely to take its place as one of the perennial forms—to use the term in its loosest and vaguest sense—of music. One may mention in particular that kind of suite which consists in the arrangement, for concert use, of music taken from stage pieces, operas and ballets, both old and new. In this connexion one thinks at once of such things as *Peer Gynt, L'Arlé-sienne, Shéhérazade, Daphnis and Chloë, Job*—all of them master-pieces of their kind, and highly characteristic of their respective composers.

IV

The Sonata, as a Whole

Students are often confused, and pardonably so, on learning that whereas 'a sonata' is a composition, usually in more than two movements, for a certain instrument or combination of instruments, the term 'sonata form' is applied as a rule to a particular type of structure, and refers only to a single movement. It is also known as 'first-movement form', and that is how it will be designated in these pages, for thus we can avoid the major confusion referred to above. Minor confusions are still possible, but not for anyone who will bear the two following points in mind:

(1) First-movement form is to be associated in time with the age of Haydn, Mozart, and their successors. It is not found (though certain features of it are sometimes foreshadowed) in the previous epoch—the epoch, that is to say, which culminated in Bach and Handel.

(2) First-movement form is by no means confined to the first movement. It is often found in the last movement also, and occasionally—though much more rarely—in the intervening movements.

The above is just a preliminary word of warning. The ground is now cleared for a general discussion of what is meant by a sonata, with reference both to the work as a whole and to the individual movements of which it is compounded. It will be convenient to subdivide this discourse into two principal sections, dealing first of all with the sonata of Bach and Handel's time (not altogether forgetting their predecessors), and then with that of the great Viennese composers. It would be an immense convenience if one could speak, *tout court,* of the 'eighteenth-century' and the 'nineteenth-century' types, but unfortunately that is impossible,

for the break comes, historically, about the middle of the eighteenth century. In future, to save circumlocution, I shall use the
antithesis of 'Bach type' and 'Beethoven type', hoping that the
explanation here given will make clear just what is indicated by
this very broad classification.

1. *The Earlier Form of the Sonata (the 'Bach type')*

It was observed in the last chapter (p. 16) that the word 'sonata'
was originally of very wide, not to say vague, significance, and
that the suite (as it afterwards came to be called) was in the first
place regarded merely as a special type of sonata—the type, that is
to say, in which dance movements predominated. The other type,
the so-called 'sonata da chiesa', with no dance movements, continued to develop on independent lines, and as the term 'sonata
da camera' fell into disuse, being replaced by the term 'suite', so
the corresponding distinction 'da chiesa' became superfluous,
and we are left simply with the suite on the one hand and the
sonata on the other.

The development of the sonata coincided very closely in time
with the development of the stringed instruments which was so
remarkable a feature of this period, and the great majority of
these earlier sonatas were written for one or more stringed
instruments, together with a keyboard accompaniment. This last
was given, as a rule, simply in the form of a figured bass, from
which the pianist (as we should now call him) was expected to
prepare or improvise the details of his accompaniment—a
delightful labour-saving process, from the composer's point of
view, but no small responsibility for the man at the keyboard.

Nowadays we limit the term 'sonata' to compositions for a keyboard solo, or for keyboard and one other instrument. When
more instruments take part, we speak of a 'trio', 'quartet', &c.,
but in the time of Corelli and the other great fiddler composers
there was no such restriction, and though a very large number of
sonatas were written for a solo violin and keyboard, there are
plenty in which two or more stringed instruments take part.
Purcell's two sets, for example—based avowedly on some Italian
model not hitherto identified with certainty—were written for two

violins, violoncello, and figured bass. Compositions for keyboard solo, however, were seldom sonatas, either in name or in form. The obvious exception, of course, is Domenico Scarlatti; but his so-called 'sonatas' are sharply distinguished, both in form and style, from all other contemporary work. They are single movements to which he chose to give the name sonata, and something will be said of their structure in the next chapter, so that they need not now be more fully described.

The commonest number of movements in a typical sonata of the earlier period is four, two slow and two fast in alternation, beginning with a slow. There are numerous exceptions, of course; Bach himself, in his Sixth Violin Sonata,[1] has his quick movements first and last, and interpolates an allemande-like movement for keyboard solo between the two slow movements, making five in all. Corelli prefers the five-movement sonata, the extra movement being frequently of the *moto perpetuo* type, to give the fiddler a chance of showing off his extra paces. Tartini, on the other hand, prefers to have three movements only—fast, slow, fast; in this respect he anticipates the practice of Haydn and Mozart, whose sonatas (unlike their symphonies) were normally of not more than three movements. It was Beethoven who brought the sonata into line with the symphony, so far as the number of movements was concerned.

In most of these movements the tonic key prevails; there is seldom more than one in any different key, and that key invariably a closely related major or minor. Of the two quick movements, one is almost always of the canzona type—i.e. the kind of freely fugued dialogue described on p. 93; but with this difference—that there is frequently a recapitulation of the opening section, so that the movement is really a composite of ternary outline and fugal texture. The recapitulation, and the resulting ternary outline, prefigure the later first-movement form; yet there is all the difference in the world between the two types. In the Bach type the movement is continuous and discursive, and unity of mood prevails throughout; in the Beethoven type, the

[1] References in this chapter to Bach's violin sonatas must be understood as applying to the six sonatas for violin and keyboard, not to those for violin solo.

themes and motives are strongly defined and contrasted with one another in rhythm, mood, and key. The Bach type might be defined as a diversified unity, the Beethoven type as a unified diversity.[2]

The other quick movement may also be of this pattern; in Bach it frequently is. Outside of Bach, it more commonly approximates to the shape of a dance movement, in that it has a double bar and repeats. But the dimensions are more ample, and neither in time nor in rhythmic detail does it necessarily exhibit the characteristics of any particular dance. Both in this and in the canzona movement the modulations are always kept within the prescribed circle of the related keys. And as many students are not so precisely informed on this point as they should be, one may perhaps be pardoned for adding that these keys are: in a major key, the relative minor, the dominant major and its relative minor, the subdominant major and its relative minor; in a minor key, the relative major, the dominant minor and its relative major, the subdominant minor and its relative major.

Of the slow movements it is more difficult, from a purely formal point of view, to give any exact account. Both in their sonatas and (as we shall see) in their concertos the early eighteenth-century composers seem to have felt that set periods and formal balance of phrase were incompatible with that freedom of expression, lyric or elegiac, which is characteristic of slow movements. To this, as to all other rules, exceptions may be found—for instance, in the opening *Siciliano* of Bach's Fourth Violin Sonata, which is a highly formalized example of binary form; or in the first movement (cantabile) of Locatelli's Fourth Sonata for the same instrument, which is in carefully constructed ternary form, the recapitulation being so altered as to emphasize the tonic and not the dominant key at the finish. But in general such formalities are avoided; unity of mood and style, a controlled plan of modulation—these are what the composer relies

[2] It should in honesty be pointed out that in Haydn's hands the first-movement form—and, for the matter of that, the rondo form too—may exhibit a highly unified and concentrated pattern. In this connexion, Tovey's article on the sonata forms in the *Ency. Brit.* is highly instructive. See also below (Ch. VI, p. 59). None the less, the antithesis is in the main a true one.

on to hold the movement together, and when he thinks he has gone on long enough, relatively to the other movements, he stops. This is true up to a point, even of Bach; but in his slow movements this unity of style and mood is usually reinforced by some persistent figure of accompaniment, maintained and adapted with most masterly skill to the shifting harmonies, which imparts the highest possible degree of cohesion to the movement as a whole. The opening largo of the Fifth (F minor) Violin Sonata may be cited here; but it is in the concertos, even more than the sonatas, that this particular aspect of his technique is best exemplified. The reader is therefore referred to Ch. VII, p. 66, for its further illustration.

Just by way of example, before passing on to the later development of the sonata, a brief descriptive analysis of one of Bach's violin sonatas—No. 3 in E major—is appended:

1. (*Adagio*) (Common time; E major). A characteristically Bachian melody of the arabesque type, with a profusion of short notes; the accompaniment is independent, and not dialogued with the violin. The principal mediate cadences are in bars 10 and 24; bars 25–34 are a very free recapitulation of bars 1–10. The whole is therefore more or less ternary, but the form is very easy and unconstrained.

2. (*Allegro*) (¢ time; E major). A free fugue in three-part counterpoint, more loosely planned, perhaps, than is usual with Bach. Two-part writing prevails throughout in the keyboard part, but the lion's share of the thematic work falls to the R.H., the L.H. having an occasional entry or piece of imitation, but for the most part an independent bass of crotchets and quavers.

3. (*Andante*) ($\frac{3}{4}$ time; C♯ minor). Like the first movement, this is ternary in outline, but without rigour of construction, the scheme being as follows:

A. (1–21) Exposition, in which the keyboard and the violin exchange roles at bar 13, the R.H. taking over the melody, and the violin the rhythmic figure of accompaniment.

B. (21–53) Development of the principal melodic units, in the form of a dialogue between the violin and the R.H. of the keyboard.

A1. (53–65) Recapitulation, considerably modified and abbreviated.

(Except for the last three bars, the L.H. of the keyboard moves persistently in crotchets, without break or modification.)

4. (*Allegro*) ($\frac{3}{4}$ time; E major). Another free fugue of the 'ternary' kind—i.e. with a recapitulation of the opening section, much on the lines of the Preludes to the English Suites in A minor and G minor. Scheme:

A. (1–35) Straightforward fugal section, consisting of the usual three-part exposition, followed by a short development and formal close.

B. (35–120) Middle section. Bars 35–78 constitute a long episode, in which two new figures make their appearance. At bar 78 these figures disappear, and the fugue resumes its normal development.

A. (121–156) Formal recapitulation of bars 1–35.

II. *The Later Form of the Sonata (the 'Beethoven type')*

Let me begin by repeating—for it is of great importance—that the analysis to be carried out in the second part of this chapter, and in the two following chapters, takes us far beyond the limits of the sonata, in the restricted sense of the term. In that sense, a sonata is still a composition for not more than two instruments; structurally, however, it is far more than that, for the principles of its organization prevail henceforward in all the major departments of orchestral and chamber music. From the analytical standpoint, a string quartet is simply a sonata for two violins, viola, and violoncello; a symphony is a sonata for full orchestra. It is purely to facilitate reference that our examples are drawn mainly from pianoforte sonatas; they could equally well have been taken from trios, quartets, and symphonies of the same school and period, and students should investigate for themselves, as far as possible, in this wider field.

The sonata, then (to resume the task of definition), is a composition sometimes of two, but more commonly of three or four movements[3]—seldom or never of more than that.[4] Of these, the first movement is commonly in first-movement form, and frequently the last as well. If the last is not in first-movement form, it is probably a rondo.[5] And both the first-movement form and the rondo form are of such intricacy and importance as to demand each a chapter to themselves. In this chapter, therefore, all we have now to consider is the minuet (or scherzo) and the slow movement. Let us take the former first.

The Minuet and Scherzo

The characteristics of the minuet as a dance form have already been described in Chapter III, and there is no need to recapitulate them here. There is a great difference of character between a Bach minuet and a Haydn one, for in Haydn's hands the minuet is continually trying (and with success) to turn itself into a scherzo. But there is no difference of a purely formal character, except that the earlier minuet—considered apart from its trio—is usually of binary construction, whereas both in Haydn and Mozart the ternary type is the normal one. The scheme is almost invariably A : ‖ : B A or A : ‖ : B A′, the variation of A being necessitated when the first A does not close in the tonic key. Usually it does, but not invariably, and when it does not, of course it has to be modified when it recurs later, in order that the final cadence of the minuet may be in the tonic. But the minuet of Haydn's quartets and symphonies is no longer a stately and graceful dance: it is whimsical, piquant, impetuous, of a lively tempo,

---

[3] Not including the Introduction (if any). This has always been an optional and (since Haydn at any rate) a somewhat unusual feature. It varies greatly both in dimensions and in structure; one cannot consider it as having any definite form.

[4] People will naturally exclaim 'What about Beethoven's posthumous quartets?' These monumental works are in many ways a law unto themselves; the boldness of their construction is appropriate to the energy and profundity of their musical thought, and their full analysis would be a monograph in itself. I must regretfully leave them outside the purview of this booklet.

[5] Not necessarily, of course. Of Beethoven's four last sonatas, op. 106 and op. 110 finish with a fugue, opp. 109 and 111 (like the 'Eroica' Symphony) with a set of variations. The finales of op. 10 (No. 2) and op. 78 do not conform to any of the regulation types. Generalizations of this kind will only mislead those who take them too literally.

abounding in abrupt rhythms and unexpected turns of phrase. The triple time and the addition of a trio enable it still to pass nominally as a minuet, but in reality it is very different. It is, in fact, a scherzo.

Beethoven saw that the time had now come when the sonata, no less than the symphony and the quartet, might be given a fourth movement, though he continued up to the very end to write sonatas also of two and three movements. But he saw also that this movement should not necessarily be a minuet, and that when it was not, there was no point in calling it so. Sometimes he calls it a scherzo, sometimes—as in the Sonatas op. 109 and 110—he does not label it at all, but simply gives the indication, 'prestissimo', 'molto allegro', or whatever it may be. In one sonata—op. 31, No. 3—a scherzo takes the place of the slow movement, and is immediately followed by a minuet and trio. In this case the scherzo is naturally not given the form of a minuet, but is cast in ordinary first-movement form—as is the somewhat similar movement in the first of the Razoumoffsky quartets.

But more often than not the Beethoven scherzo and trio is cast on the same structural lines as the minuet and trio, so that no further description of it is necessary. Sometimes (though not in the sonatas) the trio is played a second time, to be followed by yet another repetition of the scherzo itself. Beethoven's object in this, no doubt, is primarily to extend the actual duration of the scherzo, and thus give it an importance more closely approximating to that of the other movements. The method, it must be admitted, is a naïve one, and involves a certain theoretical redundancy. But what is logically wrong may be psychologically right, and music is not a process of pure thought. It is to a certain extent an art of pattern, and all pattern involves repetition in a greater or lesser degree. At any rate the incongruity (if such there be) is not unwelcome when the ideas are those of the Bb Symphony or the C# minor Quartet. We may admit, nevertheless, that the true solution of this problem is the second trio, such as we find in Dvořák's 'New World' Symphony, or Schumann's first two in Bb and C. This was one of the few discoveries that Beethoven left for his successors to make.

The Slow Movement

The slow movement is predominantly lyric, romantic, or elegiac in character, and it exhibits a greater variety of construction than any of the other movements. It is best dealt with by the method of simple enumeration:

(1) *Straightforward ternary form, with or without coda.* Quite common—especially in concertos, e.g. the violin concertos of Beethoven, Brahms, and Mendelssohn. Of Beethoven's Pianoforte Sonatas, op. 7; op. 10, No. 3 (the coda in this case is a long one, beginning at bar 65, and continuing for 25 bars more); op. 28; op. 31, No. 1.

(2) *Complete first-movement form.* This tends to prolong the slow movement unduly: yet it is by no means uncommon in Haydn and Mozart (e.g. Haydn, Pianoforte Sonatas No. 21 (E♭); 26 (E); 27 (C minor); 28 (A♭): Mozart, Pianoforte Sonatas in B♭ (K. 333); F (K. 533 and 494)). Rare in Beethoven; op. 22 is the only example in the Pianoforte Sonatas; the D major Symphony and the F major Quartet (op. 59, No. 1) also have slow movements in this form.

(3) *Abbreviated first-movement form*—i.e. with the development omitted, the return being made either direct or by a short link passage. Such a movement might reasonably be described as binary, though quite different from the binary movements found in the suite. Fairly common—e.g. Mozart, Pianoforte Sonatas in F (K. 332); String Quartets in B♭ (K. 499); B♭ (K. 589); Quintet in G minor (K. 516): Beethoven, Pianoforte Sonatas in F minor (op. 2, No. 1)[6]; C minor (op. 10, No. 1); D minor (op. 31, No. 2); Quartet in B♭ (op. 130).

(4) *Short rondo form* (A B A C A). Used both by Mozart, Pianoforte Sonatas in C minor (K. 457) and C major (K. 545); and

---

[6] Hadow (*Sonata Form,* p. 132) gives this movement as an example of simple ternary form, with coda starting at bar 48. I can't follow him here, though I should have agreed with him in describing the movement as 'one in which no controversial question should arise'. Evidently we are both of too optimistic a nature.

The recapitulation, starting at bar 32, is perfectly regular, except for the omission (for brevity's sake) of bars 17–22, and there is no coda to speak of. Or so it seems to me.

Beethoven, Pianoforte Sonatas in A (op. 2, No. 2) and C minor (op. 13); 'Harp' Quartet (op. 74).

(5) *Extended rondo form* (A B A C A B A). Rare, for the same reason that first-movement form is rare; Beethoven's Pianoforte Sonata in G (op. 31, No. 1) is sometimes given as an example, but (as I think) wrongly. The slow movement of his Fourth Symphony is an authentic example, while that of the Fifth is a blend of rondo and variation form.

(6) *Air and variations*. Again rare, so far as the pianoforte sonata is concerned; the variation form is used in several of Beethoven's sonatas, both for pianoforte alone and for pianoforte and violin, but not (in the case of the former) for the slow movement, except in op. 14, No. 2 (G major) and op. 57 (F minor). In quartets it is much commoner—see, for example, Haydn's 'Emperor' Quartet, and several of his symphonies; Mozart's Quartet in A major (K. 464) and several of Beethoven's, notably the two mighty works in E♭ (op. 127) and C♯ minor (op. 131). The slow movement of Sibelius's E♭ Symphony may also be regarded as a set of variations, albeit of an extremely subtle and elusive kind.

There is one other form of the slow movement, specially favoured by Haydn in his symphonies, which does not fall into any of the above categories, and which therefore needs a brief description. It is a sectional form in which a melodic period is succeeded by another in the opposite mode (i.e. minor if the first is major, major if the first is minor) and both—or sometimes the first only—are then repeated with embellishments and variations. As Haydn's symphonies, owing to their immense quantity, are somewhat difficult of identification by number (he has no K-list, like Mozart), I will give the themes of the opening allegros of some well-known symphonies by him in which the slow movement takes this form:

('Paukenwirbel')

Akin to this is the design of the immense slow movement of Beethoven's Ninth Symphony, in which the principal melody in B♭, after being succeeded twice by a strongly contrasted strain in two different keys (D and G), is then worked out in the form of leisurely and long-drawn-out variations to complete the movement. Of the same family, too, is the equally remarkable slow movement in the Lydian mode from the posthumous Quartet in A minor (op. 132), the formal scheme of which is as follows:

A. Long sustained melody, of an unmistakably ecclesiastical character, in the key of F, but with B♮ (the distinguishing feature of the old 'Lydian' scale). Common time.

B. Pace quickens; time changes to $\frac{3}{8}$, key to D major. Another complete and fairly long section, contrasting in the strongest possible way with A, yet mysteriously compatible with it.

A. (Varied.)

B. (Varied.)

A. (Yet another variation.)

As this is the only chapter devoted to the consideration of the sonata as a whole, it seems the most convenient place to say a few words about a device that has often been employed by composers since Beethoven's day to give greater unity to a composition—the device of a 'cyclic' theme, that is to say, a theme that reappears at intervals throughout the course of a work of several movements. This proceeding is usually associated with composers of the romantic and post-romantic periods. Foreshadows of it, however, may be found in Beethoven—e.g. in the Pianoforte Sonata, op. 101, where the opening theme of the first movement makes a brief reappearance just before the Finale; in op. 110, where the course of the final fugue is dramatically broken by the return of the earlier Arioso; in the Fifth Symphony, where the scherzo theme makes a still more dramatic irruption in the very middle of the Finale.

Later examples are not far to seek. Such things as Berlioz's 'Symphonie Fantastique' and Liszt's 'Faust' Symphony will readily occur to the mind; other composers who have used the same device to a greater or less extent are Elgar (First Symphony), Dvořák ('New World' Symphony), César Franck (String Quartet in D; Symphony in D minor); Vaughan Williams ('London' Symphony); Debussy (String Quartet in G minor). Less known, but most thoroughgoing of all, is Vincent d'Indy's String Quartet in E minor (op. 45), the four movements of which are constructed almost entirely from a group of four notes taken from a plainsong melody.

Whether a work actually gains in unity by this device of thematic transference is open to question. Unskilfully used, its effect might be just the opposite, and no one, surely, is going to suggest that Beethoven's 'Eroica' is less completely unified than his C minor, or that the symphonies of Brahms are inferior, in this respect, to the 'New World' or the 'Symphonie Fantastique'. As far as one can judge, the innovation is likely to prove less important than was at one time considered probable. Its legitimacy cannot for a moment be called in question; but, at the same time, if a composer has got sufficient inventive power, he will be able to manage perfectly well without it. At best it is useful without being essential; at worst, it might well seem factitious.

V

First-Movement Form

For the sake of clearness, it seems best to begin by defining, in the briefest possible terms, the essential outlines of this form:

It consists of three distinct and well-defined sections—the exposition, the development (otherwise known as the 'working-out' or 'free fantasia'), and the recapitulation. It is therefore, in the accepted sense of the term, ternary.

The invention of the form is usually ascribed to C. P. E. Bach; it certainly occurs in his works, and he may well be entitled to the credit of its discovery. Nevertheless it may equally well have been discovered independently by other people about the same time; there is no direct evidence, so far as I know, that Haydn 'borrowed' it from Bach, much less that Domenico Scarlatti did. Yet Scarlatti seems always to be trembling on the verge of its discovery, and once at least, in the well-known 'sonata' which begins thus:

we find what is to all intents and purposes a specimen of full-dress first-movement form, quite early-Haydnesque in design, though uncompromisingly Scarlattian in style.

This one example may be a 'sport'. Those who are interested in the evolution of form, however, should on no account overlook Scarlatti, for he, more than anyone else, is a connecting link between the old and the new. He made many experiments, but of most interest for our present purpose are those numerous movements which at a casual glance, with their double bars and repeats, look exactly like, and are usually classified as, 'binary' movements of the type normal to that period.

The difference—and it is a most important one—lies in the relation of the second half to the first. Instead of a general similarity of style, with a casual reference at the beginning and the end to the corresponding places in the first half, we find an exact repetition, in the tonic key, of most of the material of the first part. Only that which was originally in the tonic key is omitted, its place being taken by a short 'free fantasia', similar in style to the opening of the movement, and often based on figures taken therefrom.

Suppose that this 'free fantasia' had been somewhat extended; suppose further that the ensuing recapitulation had been of the entire first section, and not merely of the last two-thirds or so—obviously, in this case, the result would have been first-movement form as we know it. These are steps that might very easily have been taken, and indeed were actually taken in the one instance quoted above.

As it is, the substitution of a very short 'free fantasia' for the opening sentences leaves the two halves of approximately equal length, and one is justified in regarding these sonatas, as they stand, as examples of 'binary' rather than 'ternary' structure, despite the recapitulation in the tonic key. But they are clearly pointers to future development, and entitle their composer to rank as a figure of importance in the history of musical form.

To return to the main issue. The best plan seems to be first to take each of the principal divisions—exposition, development, recapitulation—in order by itself, and after examining them separately, to consider then what is their true relationship to one another. One begins naturally with the exposition.

1. *The Exposition*

The exposition, like the movement as a whole, is tripartite, and the function of its respective divisions is properly to be stated in terms of key:

(1) The function of the first section is to state and emphasize the tonic key. As this key prevails throughout the recapitulation, it is advisable, in order that the key system may be

well balanced, that the opening section should not be of undue length. It is normally the shortest of the three sections.

(2) The function of the second (known sometimes as the 'bridge' or 'transition') is gradually to obliterate the sense of the tonic and prepare the way for the new key that is to predominate in the third section.

(3) The function of the third section is to assert and maintain this new key, whatever it may be (this will be discussed later). Therefore, for the reasons of balance mentioned above, it is the longest of the three sections—as long as, or longer than, the other two put together.

The first section of the exposition is often known as 'principal subject', the third section as 'second subject'. These terms are thoroughly objectionable and misleading. In the first place, the term 'principal subject' suggests that the opening theme is in some way more important than the themes that occur later—a suggestion which is quite erroneous. In the second place, the term 'subject' is quite inapplicable to a complex period which consists normally of several distinct though related ideas. Many and many a time have students brought up to me, as their first essay in this form, a tune in the tonic, some haphazard bars of modulation, and another tune in the dominant, fondly imagining that this could pass for an exposition. And invariably the reason has been found to lie in this mistaken use of the word 'subject', which has given them wrong preconceptions. True that a little preliminary analysis would have and ought to have put them on their guard—but that is another story.

It is undeniable that the first section does occasionally consist of no more than a single sentence, Beethoven's op. 2, No. 1 (F minor) is a case in point—and incidentally an object lesson in the economical use of an idea. But such brevity is abnormal. Much more typical is an opening like that of op. 14, No. 1 (E major), which is concise enough in all conscience, being only twelve bars long: yet in these twelve bars we may distinguish no less than four clearly defined ideas, bars 1–4, 5–6, 7–8, 9–12 being all totally different in their melodic and rhythmical conformation, although as a whole the section gives a remarkable impression of unity and consistency. This power of unifying the diverse is really what distinguishes the art of composition from the faculty of invention; it is on this above all that the would-be composer should concentrate his fiercest endeavours.

It was said above that the structural object of this section is to define and emphasize the tonic key. This does not mean that no incidental modulations or transitions may occur; on the contrary. Indeed, one of Beethoven's favourite devices in building up this part of the movement is to repeat the opening phrase at once in a key immediately above or below the original key (Sonatas in G major (op. 31); C major (op. 53); F minor (op. 57); Quartet in E minor (op. 59); F minor (op. 95)). But the details are always so contrived that such changes of key are felt as incidental, and the prevalence of the tonic is restored by the time the end of the section is reached. In the earlier sonatas there is normally a full close to mark this point; in later times the line is not always so clearly drawn, but even in such late Beethoven sonatas as opp. 90, 106, and 110, the orthodox full close is employed to mark the end of the section.

The second, or transitional section, on the other hand, carefully avoids being too definitely in any one key. It usually begins in the old key and ends in, or within reach of, the new, but it may touch other keys in the course of its passage; indeed, you might almost say that its business is to lay false clues of this kind. As regards thematic material, it may at once inaugurate new ideas of its own (Beethoven, opp. 7, 28, 110) or proceed discursively by developing the initial idea (op. 31, No. 1 and also No. 2), or do both. The latter is perhaps the commonest; the transition first takes up an idea or unit contained in the opening section, and works forward from this starting-point into fresh territory (op. 10, No. 3, opp. 22, 53, 57). Occasionally the process is reversed, as in op. 31, No. 3, where the transition starts off with a new idea of its own, and then harks back to the opening phrase, from which the following section is then reached directly.

In any case, such new material as there may be tends to be rhythmical rather than melodic in character. The section is definitely episodic, and its transitional function should never be lost sight of; square-cut themes and formal melodic stanzas are out of place here, though they may and often do occur in the other sections.

The third section is the longest and in some ways the most important of the three. Its function is to drive home the new tonality,[1] and it takes a certain amount of time to do this with the necessary thoroughness, the more so as other subsidiary keys may also become prominent in this section—not perhaps in the case of Haydn and Mozart, but certainly in Beethoven and his successors. In the so-called 'Pathétique' Sonata, for example, the section starts in the key of E♭ minor, and passes successively through D♭ major, F minor, and C minor before the orthodox key of E♭—the relative major—is finally reached and clinched; in op. 31, No. 1 (G), the section starts in B major, and after various other keys have been suggested, the true objective turns out to be, not the orthodox D major at all, but B minor. Previous to Beethoven the invariable rule was that in this section the prevailing key should be the dominant or the relative major, and Beethoven himself abides by it, to a large extent, in his early works. Those of his middle and later periods show a much wider range of choice; in addition to the Sonata in G quoted above, one may cite as examples op. 31, No. 2, in D minor, where the second key is A minor instead of F major; op. 53, in C (E major instead of G major); op. 106, in B♭ (G major instead of F major), and so on. Such examples could easily be multiplied, both from Beethoven himself and from his successors, notably Brahms. Generally speaking, the keys of the mediant and submediant have been added to the previous list of dominants and relatives; more remote keys than this have been eschewed, as also the key of the subdominant. Nor are these ever likely now to come into favour; modern experiments are taking a totally different direction, and the very idea of enlarging the key system seems a trifle ridiculous in these days, when key itself has so

---

[1] In his major movements—not his minor ones—Haydn commonly starts the section by repeating his opening theme in the dominant key. This entry seems redundant, and is never found in later composers.

nearly disappeared—though whether that disappearance be for ever, who can say?

As regards the thematic construction of this section, one can only say, generally, that, like the other two, it is a complex of various contrasting themes and ideas. Its full possibilities were not realized all at once; in Haydn and Mozart—especially in their earlier works—something is often felt to be lacking. Thematic invention is to some extent replaced by what might be described comprehensively as 'passage work'—a 'plebeian retinue'[2] of scales and arpeggios, employed, for want of something better, to eke out the section to the length required. But this is not true of their best works, any more than it is true of Beethoven and the other great composers who used this form. Two features are worthy of special mention:

(1) One at least of the themes in this section is commonly a broad melodic stanza—a tune, in fact—that both contrasts with and stabilizes the more energetic and restless rhythmical parts. (It is always such a theme that people have in mind when they speak of the 'second subject'. Subject, yes, but why 'second'? And why apply to a whole section a term that properly designates only a single theme in that section?)

It is hardly necessary to give examples of so very common a feature; think, if you will, of the A♭ major melody of the 'Appassionata', or the E major one of the 'Waldstein'.

(2) Where the exposition closes with a double bar and repeat, a short coda is often required, as the real close of the section is of course made in the new key, and the immediate restart in the old key, without such intervention, might sound abrupt (op. 10, No. 3, illustrates). The alternative is to have two continuations, one leading to the return, the other to the development section which follows, as in op. 78.

These three sections together, then, constitute what is known as the exposition. Next in order to be considered is the development.

---

[2] Hadow's felicitous description.

2. *The Development*

The relation of the development to the other two sections, and the part it plays in the scheme as a whole, will be discussed at the end of this chapter. What concerns us here and now is to find out in detail what the term denotes, what actually happens when a composer sets out to 'develop' one of his themes. There are various methods of development, and they may be enumerated as follows. Be it noted that the examples cited are not necessarily taken from the 'development section' of the given work. For the most part they are, but 'development' often occurs in other sections than the one specifically so called, and it really does not matter what section the examples come from, so long as they serve to illustrate the particular point at issue.

(1) A theme, or a unit of a theme, may simply be extended melodically by continuing it in an upward or downward direction.

This is a rare method, for purely melodic developments are seldom successful, and themes that lend themselves to such treatment are few. But a glance through the development of the first movement of Brahms's Second Symphony will show what can be done with it when circumstances are favourable. A brief quotation follows for the benefit of those who have not a score handy:

And again, some 60 bars later:

(2) The above also illustrates in simple fashion another available resource—that of melodic inversion. Apart from its frequent employment in fugue (see p. 106), this common device supplies familiar continuations in music of quite other kinds; see, for example, the opening of the fourth number of Brahms's German Requiem ('How lovely is Thy dwelling-place'), the Scherzo of his Fourth Symphony (bar 35), the Scherzo of Beethoven's Seventh (bar 99), and elsewhere.

(3) Melodic outline may be kept, but the rhythm altered. See, for example, the opening of the development section of Beethoven's 'Sonata pathétique', where the first phrase of the introduction appears in this guise:

(4) The same device may be used without adhering strictly to the original melodic intervals, provided there is some characteristic leap or curve that secures recognition. Here is the opening theme of Debussy's String Quartet, and some of the transformations it undergoes in the course of the work:

No less entertaining and instructive are the transformations in the third movement—a minuet and scherzo combined—of Brahms's Second Symphony:

(5) The subject may be treated contrapuntally in various ways. A simple counter melody works wonders in Beethoven's Fourth Symphony:

In his D major Sonata (op. 28) the treatment is by double counterpoint of a somewhat more elaborate character (see the passage that starts at the 21st bar after the double bar). In the great B♭ Sonata (op. 106) the development starts with an elaborate fugato, while in the Finale of the A major Sonata (op. 101) a complete though very free fugue replaces the normal methods of development.

(6) Change of mode (major for minor or vice versa) and change of harmony may be taken as a matter of course—not so much as being in themselves methods of development, but rather as an almost inevitable corollary and accompaniment of other methods.

(7) Some characteristic unit or rhythmic figure from one of the subjects is taken and made the basis of an extended passage, the treatment being by dialogue, or by sequence, or any way the composer can devise, provided the characteristic rhythm or

configuration is preserved closely enough to remain recognizable. This is too common to need specific reference; it is the most generally serviceable of all the methods.

Such treatment, in the hands of a skilful composer, never gives the effect of aimless or haphazard modulation. Passages constructed in this manner are always felt, in Beethoven most of all, as working towards a definite end—either a dynamic climax, or the introduction of one of the other themes in a new and unexpected key, or the turn homeward that prepares for the recapitulation, or whatever it may be.

(8) The use of new material in the development section has never been regarded by composers as outside the law, whatever theorists may say. The famous E minor episode in the 'Eroica' Symphony does not stand by itself. In Beethoven's Pianoforte Sonata in E♭ (op. 7), in a very similar place, there appears quite a new little theme in (of all keys in the world) A minor. In the E major Sonata (op. 14, No. 1), the greater part of the development is built up from a figure that is not derived from any of the foregoing thematic material. In the C major (op. 2, No. 3) the most important part of the development—that which starts with the entry of the opening theme in D major—is preceded by a dozen bars or so of broken arpeggios whose function is not thematic at all, but purely harmonic and dynamic. Much the same thing happens in op. 10, No. 2, and (on a vastly larger scale) in op. 57, where a wrathful cascade of arpeggios brings the development to its conclusion.

Regarding the last paragraph, a word of warning to the would-be composer may not be out of place. If such new material is introduced because the composer feels that just that, and nothing else, is appropriate at that particular juncture, well and good. If he is driven to introduce it because he cannot devise satisfactory continuations from the material already to hand, it is far from well; his craftsmanship is at fault. Let the young composer appeal to the precedent of Beethoven by all means, but let him also not forget the saying, 'Quod licet Jovi, non licet bovi'. On this point especially must he be absolutely honest with himself.

No specimen of detailed analysis follows here. With the help of what has been said, and the references already given, the student should have no difficulty in seeing for himself how the various methods just enumerated are combined and worked out in practice. Once more, his researches need not and should not be restricted to the comparatively narrow field of the pianoforte sonata; but within that field I would suggest especially the developments of Beethoven's op. 2, No. 2 (A major) and op. 14, No. 2 (G major) among the early sonatas; op. 28 (D major), op. 53 (C major), op. 57 (F minor), and the last movement of op. 101 (A major), among the later ones, as being worthy of close study, not only for their intrinsic skill and excellence, but as contrasts in method.

The question is often asked, Should the development embrace all the subjects, or most of them, or only one or two? Anyone who will take the trouble to examine the half-dozen movements just suggested will be able to answer that question for himself, especially if he adds to the list the development sections in the first movements of Beethoven's Third and Eighth Symphonies. He will also be in a position to confirm Hadow's very just observation that Beethoven's developments usually start either with the opening theme of the first section or the final theme of the last.

There is just one other point worth mentioning here, and that is this: when there is no double bar and repeat of the exposition, the development is sometimes prefaced by a restatement, in the tonic key, of the opening bars. Hadow cites, *inter alia*, Brahms's Second and Third Violin Sonatas (opp. 100 and 108) and his Pianoforte Trio in C minor (op. 101); to which I would add his 'Tragic' Overture, his Fourth Symphony (op. 98), and the last movement of his first (op. 68); also the last movements of Beethoven's Eighth Symphony (op. 93), and F minor Quartet (op. 95). The idea clearly is to let the listener know just where he is; the development which follows is not in any way affected. One incidental result of this procedure is to make the first movement so like in outline to a certain type of rondo that on occasion the two are scarcely to be distinguished. More will be said on this count in the next chapter.

3. *The Recapitulation and Coda*

So far as thematic content goes the recapitulation is bound to be more or less the same as the exposition, otherwise it would not be a recapitulation. But just as the function of the exposition is to assert two principal contrasting keys, so that of the recapitulation is to show that in the final issue there can be but one paramount key—the tonic. The third section therefore must be reproduced in that key; how is this to be contrived?

(1) In the older works the transitional section frequently ended on the dominant chord, after which the new section could be introduced equally well in the dominant or the tonic. Both progressions sounded quite easy and natural, and the recapitulation could therefore be quite a literal one, with no change except this change of key.

(2) By starting the recapitulation in the subdominant instead of the tonic, it is obvious that an exact repetition would automatically bring about the entry of the third section in the tonic key. Mozart does this in his Pianoforte Sonata in C (K. 545) and Schumann in the Finale of his Pianoforte Concerto. But I can recall no other instance; composers seem to have felt instinctively that this cutting of the knot was hardly fair.

(3) Failing these too simple devices, the composer is clearly left with the necessity of modifying something somewhere, and that something is usually the transitional section. The device employed varies with each individual work; sometimes (as in Beethoven's op. 2, No. 1) the alteration is of the simplest kind necessary to effect the change of key required; sometimes (as in op. 110 and even more in op. 106) most extensive modifications are made, and quite remote keys temporarily established, so that the final supremacy of the tonic is only vindicated after a further prolonged struggle.

In itself, the tendency of such manœuvres is to lengthen the recapitulation (as compared with the exposition) rather than to curtail it. But there are many works in which the recapitulation is abbreviated by the omission of part—or even the whole—of one

of the sections. Clearly, in such a case, the themes that can best
be dispensed with are those that have been prominent in the
development, or are going to become so in the coda. Beethoven's
op. 31, No. 1 and No. 2, both afford excellent examples; so does
Brahms's Second Symphony. It is the intermediate section, as a
rule, that is thus cut short; but on occasion the opening section
itself is omitted, as in Chopin's B minor and B♭ minor Pianoforte
Sonatas, also in Brahms's 'Tragic' Overture, and the last movement of his First Symphony. This seems logical in cases where (as
here) the opening theme has already been repeated immediately
before the development, in the manner already described (see
p. 51). And in this context one cannot refrain from mentioning
Brahms's felicitous expedient in his Second Symphony—that
compendium of happy devices—in which the opening theme

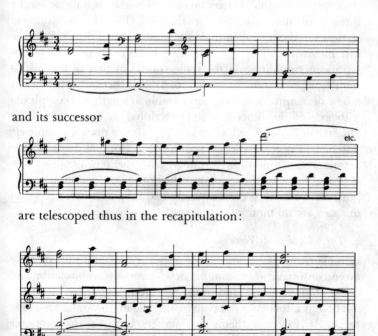

and its successor

are telescoped thus in the recapitulation:

The coda is in a sense optional. Mozart hardly ever writes one in his sonatas, and neither he nor Haydn ever regarded it as an independent and vital part of the structure. The contrapuntal virtuosity which ends the 'Jupiter' Symphony is quite a special case; the whole movement is a unique combination of contrapuntal texture with first-movement form, and the coda is, structurally, the logical climax of the whole. Generally speaking, the pre-Beethoven coda was no more than a final flourish of trumpets (I speak metaphorically). But since Beethoven it has had a very different status. In such an early work as his op. 2, No. 3, the coda is of imposing dimensions, and though one can find later movements in which there is no coda (e.g. op. 10, No. 2), one can certainly say of his first movements collectively that the coda is an essential feature, an epilogue that serves to round off the structure as a whole. It may be short or it may be long; it may be formed of new material, or founded, like the development section, on themes taken from the main body of the work. In the first movement of op. 31, No. 2, it is no more than a few subterranean rumblings on the tonic chord; in that of the 'Waldstein', and even more in that of op. 81 ('L'Absence'), it is virtually a new development section comparable in length and complexity with any of the other principal sections; in the Finale of the Quartet in F minor (op. 95) it is a diaphanous presto, completely different in time, in tempo, and in mood from all that has gone before. You can no more formulate any general principle of construction for it than for the introduction or the development. Its purpose is to clinch the matter, and so long as it is felt to do so one can ask no more of it.

4. The Scheme as a Whole

It remains to say a few words about the relationship of these three constituents—exposition; development; recapitulation and coda—to one another and to the scheme in its entirety.

There is a tendency today to belittle the importance of a theme *per se*. 'It is not the theme that matters, but what the composer makes of it'—such is the kind of remark that one constantly hears. In other words, the only part of a first movement that really counts is the development section; the exposition is merely the text of a discourse which the development provides, while the recapitulation is an outworn and otiose convention.

Whatever truth there may be in this view today—and I shall presently try to show that it is a misguided one—it certainly has no historical justification. What Haydn, Mozart, and all the rest of them had to write first of all was the exposition, of which an essential feature was the distribution of contrasting tonalities. The ultimate goal, the crowning part of the whole structure, was the recurrence of this material in a single key, which must of course be the tonic. Obviously this recurrence would be more effective if delayed for a time, especially if the exposition itself had been repeated as far as the double bar, as was invariably the case in the earlier sonatas and symphonies.

Therefore something must intervene, and that something is what we now know as the development section. But, as we have already seen, a development section does not always consist exclusively of 'development'; the composer always reserved the right to introduce new material at his discretion. Only it was clearly more economical—and to that extent more artistic—to utilize the resources already to hand, and development accordingly became the rule, new material the exception. But, in either event, the whole purpose and *ratio essendi* of the section was to prepare for and heighten the effect of the recapitulation. Mozart, for one, declined, as a rule, to take it too seriously, and the idea of development for development's sake would certainly have made him smile. Haydn and Beethoven clearly took more interest in the process, and were at pains to give this part of the movement a status and dignity of its own. But they no more than Mozart would have admitted that a theme exists in order to be 'developed'. If this were so, few indeed would be the themes to find salvation, for it is only one or two of them, as a rule, that are selected for such treatment.

The heresy is due, I think, to pressing an analogy too far. Music, like speech, exists not in space, but in time; it has from its earliest days been intimately linked with speech, which is the expression of thought. Hence one has come naturally to think and speak of music itself as a kind of thought-process, forgetting that in so doing one is employing a metaphor. For the 'thought' in music is not conceptual as is the thought which we express in language; it is 'thought' of a purely musical kind, which unfolds in accordance with the laws of its own nature, which are quite peculiar to itself and not really comparable with any other process.

You may say—and up to a point, with truth—that music, like spoken thought, has a logic of its own; but you may say with equal truth that, like architecture, it has its own formal symmetry, and that a first movement shorn of its recapitulation is mutilated as surely as York Minster would be if one of its western towers were removed. In either case, you are speaking metaphorically, and though metaphors may be suggestive and illuminating, they do not convey the whole truth or the plain truth. And the plain truth about music is that hitherto it has always admitted and depended on repetition in one form or another. 'Development' itself is for the most part repetition, with some variation, of a single pattern, a minute pattern of notes rhythmically ordered. 'Recapitulation' is the repetition, also with some variation, of the much larger and more complex pattern displayed in the exposition. From a purely intellectualist standpoint it may seem at first sight to be dispensable, but without it the foreordained scheme of key distribution cannot be fulfilled in its entirety. It is therefore an essential part of the design as a whole.

Where key distribution is not considered of primary importance, or where key is dispensed with altogether (as in so much modern music), of course the case is totally different. In this connexion it is worth while to consider, as a speculation, whether one might be able to dispense, not with the recapitulation, but with the exposition. In this case the design would somewhat resemble the plot of a detective story; fragments of the themes would be presented first of all, one after another being gradually brought under notice, given its due meed of emphasis and then withdrawn, much as the various clues and threads of the mystery are presented, obtrusively or otherwise, to the attentive reader. As the work progressed various connexions and combinations would begin to appear, until finally the whole solution would be unmasked, and the *disjecta membra* of the earlier stages firmly knit together and presented to the listener in the form of a clear and continuous exposition (or recapitulation—it does not matter which you call it). It would not be an easy method, either for the composer or for the listener, from whom close concentration and even memorization would be required in order to grasp the design at a single hearing. But though difficult, it would seem, *a priori*, to be perfectly feasible. Constant Lambert claims, indeed (in *Music Ho!*), that it has actually been practised by Sibelius in certain of his symphonic movements. This, I think, is going rather farther than the facts warrant; but I should be the first to agree that any composer wishing to experiment on these lines would find much of Sibelius's work to be highly stimulating and suggestive.

VI

Rondo Form

The rondo, like the simple binary and ternary forms, is one that was borrowed originally from vocal music and adapted later for instrumental purposes. In the song with chorus, to be repeated at the end of each verse, you have the crude essentials of the rondo, the chorus being of course the rondo theme. The only difference is that a rondo invariably starts off with its principal theme, and when a song *begins* with a chorus—the Skye boat-song, for example—it is a true vocal rondo, neither more nor less. Some of the earlier instrumental rondos—those of Couperin, for example—conform to this primitive pattern; there is no fixed number of episodes and thematic recurrences, any more than there is a fixed number of verses in a song.

But as a matter of general practice, the rondo as we know it exists in two forms, which may be diagrammatically set out as follows:

(1) A B A C A

(2) A B A C A B A

A, of course, represents the principal theme, B and C the episodes. The first of these is usually known as 'short rondo form', the second as 'sonata rondo form'. The latter description is not happily chosen; if used at all, it should be reserved for those rondos in which the central episode (C), instead of being constructed from new material, is a development, on first-movement lines, of material taken from the earlier sections. It is much better to speak simply of the shorter and longer forms of the rondo, for in this there can be no ambiguity.

Let us now try and discover what the above diagrams really represent, beginning with the first.

1. *The Shorter Rondo Form*

Imprimis, what does A stand for? What sort of theme is suitable for a rondo, and how does it differ, if at all, from the opening theme of a first movement?

Hadow's choice of words to define the distinction could not be bettered: 'The subjects of a Rondo, particularly the first, are generally of a more simple and ballad-like character than those of a Ternary movement [i.e. one in the first-movement form]. Indeed, the first subject of a Rondo is nearly always a square-cut melodic stanza, while that of a Ternary movement is usually analysable into separate sections, of which only some are distinctly melodious.'

The only point one might criticize in this description is the suggestion that a rondo subject is not analysable into constituent sections, for the example which follows—the opening subject of the last movement of Beethoven's op. 7—is in itself a complete ternary period. What Hadow really means to emphasize is not the separateness or otherwise of the sections but (in the case of the rondo) their uniformly melodious character; he is careful to add, moreover, that this rule, like all others, has its exceptions.

Two points should be noted before passing on to consider the episodes:

(1) It is a cardinal principle of rondo form that each recurrence of the principal subject should be in the tonic key.

(2) The principal subject may recur in its exact original form, or with simple ornaments and embroideries, the latter method of presentation being the commoner.

Of the episodes, one cannot speak so precisely. Sometimes—as in the slow movement of Beethoven's Sonata in C minor (op. 13)—they are themselves hardly less melodic in character and symmetrical in construction than the main subject itself. Sometimes—as in the Finale of Haydn's Symphony in E♭ (No. 103, 'Paukenwirbel')—they are developed with so vigorous a logic from the characteristic figures of the opening theme that one can scarcely draw lines of division at all; the resultant effect is one of fierce concentration and continuity most unlike the amiable discursiveness that one usually associates with this form. Between such extremes various degrees of mean are naturally possible; but they will be found inclining, as a rule, much more to the first of the above types than to the second.

As to key, the first episode normally centres round the dominant or relative major; the second is frequently cast in the tonic minor or major (as the case may be). It thus contrasts both with the principal subject and the first episode without wandering too far afield.

2. *The Longer Rondo*

This is simply a prolongation of the shorter rondo, as the diagram suggests. After the second return of the principal subject, the first episode is repeated in the tonic key, and then comes yet one more repetition ('positively the last appearance') of the rondo theme.

There is a widespread impression that Beethoven invented this form of the rondo. Anyone who takes the trouble to analyse the last movements of Mozart's Pianoforte Sonatas in B♭ (K. 333) and F (K. 494 and 533) will see for himself that this is not the case; in each of these the scheme is unmistakably that of the longer rondo, and each movement is still further lengthened by the interpolation of a cadenza-like passage before the last appearance of the principal subject. What one may say truthfully, in respect of rondo form, is that Beethoven did nothing in the way of innovation, but a great deal in the way of clarification. Haydn and Mozart allow themselves great freedom in their rondo movements, whose detailed analysis may occasionally present some difficulty to one who approaches them with too fixed a preconception of what rondo form ought to be. Beethoven is more methodical; his principal episode in particular is more carefully planned, and there is never any doubt, at any given moment, of one's exact whereabouts.

It has already been pointed out (p. 59) that Haydn, in his E♭ Symphony, had the idea of constructing a rondo without episodes —i.e. one in which a continuous thematic development replaces the usual free kind of episode. Somewhat similar is the finale of

Mozart's Pianoforte Sonata in A minor (K. 345); it is true that the central episode in A major stands out in sharp contrast to its surroundings, but the rest of the Finale is constructed mono-thematically—to use Aubyn Raymar's description[1]—from a single figure, ♩ ♪, which dominates the entire movement. This is quite foreign to Beethoven's method; for him an episode is an episode, and it is vital to his scheme that the principal episode, which is to be repeated later in the tonic key, should both be clearly defined in itself, and sufficiently contrasted with the opening rondo theme. But he does frequently dispense with the central episode and substitute therefor a development section, in which the methods employed are precisely similar to those used in the development of an ordinary first movement. Examples may be seen in the pianoforte sonatas in B♭ (op. 22), G (op. 31, No. 1), and E (op. 90), also in the G major and E♭ piano concertos, and the E minor Quartet (op. 59, No. 2).

It is evident that such a scheme does approximate very closely on paper to that of a first movement, especially one in which there is no double bar and in which the development is preceded by a short restatement of the opening theme, in the manner described on p. 50. Consider the two schemes side by side, remembering that the principal episode in a rondo by Beethoven or Brahms is comparable, in length and complexity, with the later sections of a first movement exposition:

First Movement	*Rondo*
(1) First section in tonic key.	(1) Principal rondo theme.
(2) Transition, leading to	(2) First episode in contrasted key, preceded frequently by some sort of transitional passage.
(3) Third section in contrasted key.	
(4) Repetition of all or part of first section.	(3) Repetition of principal theme.
(5) Development.	(4) Development.
(6) Recapitulation of 1, 2, and 3 in tonic key.	(5) Recapitulation of 1 and 2 in tonic key.

[1] His introduction and annotations in the Associated Board's specially prepared edition of Mozart's pianoforte works are models of accurate scholarship and lucid analysis.

First Movement	*Rondo*
(7) Coda.	(6) Final appearance of principal subject, often so freely handled and extended as to give it the aspect of a coda.

A similar tabulation, though somewhat more abbreviated, is given in § 102 of Hadow's *Sonata Form*, with the following comment: 'It is quite possible that a movement might be written with such misplaced ingenuity as to be exactly on the border-line, and to be incapable of any certain classification. But, as a matter of practice, the great masters have kept the two forms distinct.'

Generally speaking, they have; but there is one well-known movement which—leaving aside the question of misplaced ingenuity—does seem to me to be exactly on the border-line. I refer to the last movement of Mozart's D major Pianoforte Sonata (K. 576).

Hadow himself (op. cit. § 85) classifies it as a first-movement structure in which the development is preceded by a repetition of the opening subject.

Raymar says that it 'combines features of plan of both the rondo and the sonata on a monothematic basis'.

No movement could be more logically constructed, or (in a sense) easier to analyse; but no movement could be harder to label with any dogmatic certainty. I have always thought of it myself as a rondo with developments instead of episodes, because I suspect that if Mozart had planned at the outset to give it first-movement form, there would have been a double bar somewhere. Possibly he started with one scheme in view, and then changed his mind as he went along. No one can say for certain, nor does it greatly matter.

VII

The Concerto

Part I. The Concerto in Bach and Handel's Time

'Concerto', like 'sonata', is a term which was used first in a very vague and general sense, but ultimately narrowed down into something comparatively definite and precise. Moreover, the early eighteenth-century concerto and its Mozartian successor differed from each other in no less degree than did the respective sonatas of the corresponding periods. The term seems to have been first used by Viadana, whose *Concerti Ecclesiastici* were published in 1602. These were not even instrumental compositions at all, but motets with an organ accompaniment, and it is plain that the inventor of the title was employing it, as was quite natural, in its purely etymological sense of 'joint effort'. It was soon transferred and restricted to instrumental as opposed to vocal music; but for a long time to come it remained vague in connotation, and for the greater part of the seventeenth century it would have been hard to define the precise difference between concerto and sonata. But by the beginning of the eighteenth century, at any rate,[1] a concerto had come to be a composition in which certain passages were to be played by a solo instrument or a group of soloists (the 'concertino') as contrasted with others (the 'tutti') in which all the performers took part. This idea of contrast between 'solo' and 'tutti' has ever since been part of the definition of a concerto, even to the present day, when it would be hard to give any more exact indication of what the word implies. The concerto today is not, in the strict sense of the term, a 'form' of music; it is a *genre* or medium. But that, as the reader will have gathered, might equally well be said of the sonata and the

---

[1] Corelli's *Concerti Grossi* (his last work) were published in 1712.

symphony; set forms of music are hardly in keeping with our chaotic and discordant age.

The two great representative figures of the early eighteenth century are of course Bach and Handel, and this summary discussion of the earlier concerto form must necessarily centre round their work. But one must never lose sight of the truth that 'the greatest genius is the most indebted man', and it would be ungracious not to give passing mention to others, such as Corelli and Vivaldi, who were before them in this field. It is true that after perusing their works, and comparing them mentally with those of Bach and Handel, what strikes one first is not the immense indebtedness of the latter, but their immense superiority. But the pioneer should always be given his meed of honour, and we may believe that Bach would have been among the first to acknowledge his particular debt to Vivaldi, of whose concertos he made a large number of elaborate transcriptions. The ritornello, for instance, whose importance in this connexion is so justly stressed by Tovey, is a prominent feature in most of Vivaldi's first movements; and though Vivaldi cannot claim to be the inventor of the ritornello, the use he makes of it is very striking, and probably suggested to Bach the draft outlines of his own opening movements. Of this more anon.

Before proceeding to examine the Bachian concerto in detail, let this be observed: that the dominant motive of the older concerto is *not* a display of virtuosity. It is primarily contrast of tone—and if anyone does not realize what a surprising contrast there is between the tone of a string tutti and that of a string solo (or group of solos), let him take the first opportunity of hearing Elgar's 'Introduction and Allegro' or Vaughan Williams's 'Fantasia on a Theme by Thomas Tallis'. The result, one may say with confidence, will be illuminating. And at the same time we may remind ourselves that the orchestras of Bach's and Handel's day were not the highly trained professional companies to which we are now accustomed. Much of the tutti playing must have been of a rough-and-ready nature, and this fact in itself would serve to heighten the tonal contrast of the solo passages. For though these latter call for no outstanding virtuosity of technique, they need to be really well played, and there is no reason to doubt that they were really well played.

Bach's concertos fall into two main groups—the Brandenburg Concertos, which are really 'concerti grossi', being written for soloists in groups of various kinds, and the concertos for violin and clavier, which are mostly for a single soloist, or for a pair. The former are somewhat more varied in form, for the form is bound to be influenced, in matters of detail, by the medium. But there is no essential difference of outline, and one may say generally that a Bach concerto consists of three movements, of which the middle one is slow, the other two quick. One may say further that in the quick movements the keystone of the construction is usually the ritornello, in the slow, the ground bass—using that term in a somewhat elastic sense which will presently be explained.

The ritornello form has something in common both with the rondo and the fugue, inasmuch as it consists of an essential something which recurs periodically with episodes in between. That something is the ritornello itself. It differs from the rondo in that its recurrences are not necessarily in the same key; from the fugue, in being a fully harmonized musical period, and not merely a theme; from both, in that it is associated, alike in the aria and concerto forms, with the orchestral tutti. The simplest form of it is the ritornello that happens also to be a rondo—e.g. the Finale of Bach's E major Concerto, in which the tutti always join in the ritornello (which is heard five times in all, every time in E major), while the intervening episodes are given to the solo, for whom the tutti provide the lightest of accompaniments. Analysis of the first movement will show that a ritornello movement may also, incidentally, be in strict ternary form, for in this, after the middle section has closed somewhat melodramatically with a cadence in G sharp minor, an abrupt return is made to the opening and the first 52 bars are repeated *verbatim*. But the structure is not normally of so rigid a type; the essential feature of it is simply the periodic recurrence of the ritornello, in whole or in part, played in various related keys by the tutti, with episodes in between in which the solo or group of soloists has the main share of the work. These episodes may consist of entirely fresh material, or may develop ideas contained in the ritornello itself. Few, if any, of Bach's concerto movements will present any serious analytical difficulty to one who keeps this general scheme in mind. Naturally the 'Brandenburgs', with their variously constituted concertino groups, have to be more adaptable than the clavier and the violin concertos, in which the line of cleavage between 'solo' and 'tutti' is always clearly cut. In the third and sixth of the Brandenburgs, for example, there is no tutti existing apart from the concertino; the interplay is between the different string groups, which function individually as concertino and in combination as tutti. In the first, the power of the concertino—two horns, three oboes, bassoon, and violino piccolo—is sufficient to give the tutti a good even game, so to speak, and the first and third movements are in consequence more definitely orchestral in character than in any of the other five concertos. In the fourth, on the other hand, where the concertino is only a solo violin and two flutes à bec, the tutti is handled with much more restraint, and even in the ritornello itself the concertino predominates. But in all of them—and even in the so-called 'Italian' Concerto, for clavier solo without accompaniment of any kind —the main structural outlines (of ritornello punctuated by episodes) are easily traced, at any rate in the opening movements. The finales are less uniform; that of the third is a straightforward 'binary' movement, while those of the fourth and fifth are freely fugal.

It has already been said that throughout the period we are now considering—say 1650 to 1750—composers seem to have deliberately avoided any set formal arrangement in laying out their slow movements. This is as true of the concerto as of the sonata, and it applies to Bach as well as to his contemporaries. Bach, however, differs markedly from the others in that he does not rely wholly on consistency of mood and style to give the unity that every movement should have. He reinforces it, as a rule, by consistently employing what was designated above (p. 65) as a ground bass. By this is meant, not a true 'ground' of the type described in Chapter VIII (p. 74), but a persistently recurrent figure which adapts itself from bar to bar in accordance with the harmonic requirements of the melody, but continues unchanged in rhythmic pattern. It is a curiously simple and at the same time a curiously impressive device; one sees exactly how it is done, yet it never fails to produce on one that quasi-hypnotic effect at which Bach was aiming. In some of his rapid movements the incessant regular pounding of the bass acts on many listeners as an irritant, but I have met few indeed who do not willingly surrender to the spell of this slow measured monotony, so soothing and yet so relentless. Readers will recall at once such figures as this:

from the Violin Concerto in A minor, or this:

from that in E major, or this:

from the 'Italian' Concerto.

Above this ostinato there is almost always a melody of the characteristic Bachian type, highly elaborate and rococo, with frequent groups of demisemiquavers and even lesser notes, abounding in mordents, appoggiaturas, and such-like ornamentation, subservient to no metrical pattern, but pausing to cadence only as and when the spirit moves it. The medium does not matter; be it oboe or violin, the human voice or the human hand on the keyboard, in a slow movement it has got to sing, and to sing in this elaborately lyrical style that Bach has made his own. And all the while, with occasional pauses, the basses far below pursue their own unrelenting course. No one else has ever done anything quite like it; if Bach had written nothing else but these slow movements, his immortality would have been assured.

Handel's treatment of the form is very different. Apart from the early 'oboe' concertos (so called), he wrote both solo concertos and concerti grossi, and so did Bach; but there the resemblance ends. The solo concertos are for the organ, and are said to have been written[2] largely in connexion with his oratorios —presumably for performance as interludes. Apart from the conjunction of organ and orchestra (for which there is really very little to be said), these are not works of the first magnitude. They are lively and well turned out, but I doubt if anyone would seriously claim that they are more than that. The concerti grossi, on the other hand, show Handel's genius most imposingly. Their emotional range is wide, and they display superb ease of style and mastery of form.[3] But though they are fully the equal of the Brandenburg Concertos in artistic value, they are quite differently laid out. In the former case, the concertino is always varied, so that each Brandenburg, by virtue of the medium alone, is different from its neighbours. In Handel's concertos, the lay-out is always for strings—a string tutti, diversified by episodes for two solo violins and a violoncello. In compensation, however, there is much more variety of form in Handel's work than in Bach's. With the exception of the first (to which a minuet and trios are added as a sort of afterthought), the Brandenburgs are all in three-movement form—quick movements of the ritornello or free fugal type first and last, with a slow movement in the middle. Handel prefers to have four, five, or even six movements, and his partiality for a dance movement of a lighter type to end with shows that the French overture was never very far from his

---

[2] R. A. Streatfield, *Handel,* p. 334.

[3] I cannot refrain from quoting Handel's biographer in this connexion: 'To modern ears the instrumental music of the early eighteenth century is now obsolete, and a certain amount of preliminary study is necessary before its meaning can be thoroughly grasped. . . . They [Handel and R. Strauss] seem as far apart as Chaucer from Browning. . . . In Handel's case no less than in Chaucer's the labour of mastering the dialect in which he wrote brings its own reward' (Streatfield, op. cit., p. 326). I do not think Mr. Streatfield was trying to be funny; but this idea that Handel wrote in a 'dialect' which can only be mastered by exhausting study seems to me the most comical fantasy.

thoughts. The best way to illustrate these general statements will be to append the skeleton outline of two or three of the concertos:

1. No. 3 in E minor.
   1. Short introductory larghetto, of what may be called the stock Handelian type in $\frac{3}{2}$ time (E minor).
   2. A short double fugue, with no important episodes, and no solo work, apart from a couple of passages for the 'cello. E minor; $\frac{12}{8}$ time.
   3. A most rumbustious and typically Handelian allegro of the ritornello type. E minor; common time.
   4. A longish 'Polonaise' in so-called 'binary' form, but not consistently keeping the character of the dance. G major; $\frac{3}{4}$ time.
   5. A short and sprightly movement, in $\frac{6}{8}$ time (E minor), to finish with. More or less—but rather less than more —of the A : ‖ B A type.
2. No. 5 in D major.
   1. Pompous introduction. D major; $\frac{3}{4}$ time.
   2. Lively canzona. D major; $\frac{4}{4}$ time.
   3. Presto in 'binary' form. D major, $\frac{3}{8}$ time.
   4. Introductory largo, of the 'stock' type—i.e. in $\frac{3}{2}$ time (B minor).
   5. Allegro, of the ritornello type. D major; common time.
   6. Minuet. D major, in free sectional form.

It will be noticed that these movements, grouped as indicated, virtually form two complete French overtures of orthodox pattern.

3. No. 6 in G minor.
   1. Introductory largo, of the 'stock' $\frac{3}{2}$ type (G minor, with a half close).
   2. Short four-part fugue, with no solo episodes, on a very fine chromatic subject. G minor; common time.
   3. So-called 'musette' (larghetto) in somewhat casual rondo form, the episodes being of very unequal length. E♮ major; $\frac{3}{4}$ time.

4. Ritornello movement, allegro. G minor; common time.

5. Short and lively 'binary' movement. G minor; $\frac{3}{8}$ time.

It is really the indiscriminate zeal of our contemporary Bach-worshippers that causes these fine works to be almost completely neglected today, when a concert hall can be filled with an audience prepared to listen to a programme consisting of all the Brandenburg Concertos one after the other. Fine as they are in certain respects, six off the reel is altogether too much of a good thing. I am not advocating a programme of six Handel concertos either; but why cannot our concert-givers distribute their favours a little more justly and reasonably?

Part II. *The Concerto of Mozart and his Successors*

The later form of the concerto can be described more briefly than the earlier; not because the form itself is less complex or less interesting, and still less because the concertos of Mozart, Beethoven, Brahms, and the rest, are inferior in value and importance to those of their predecessors, but simply because the form is in all essential respects so very similar to that of the sonata, which has already been fully described. A Beethoven concerto is much more like a Beethoven sonata than a Bach or Handel concerto is like a Bach or Handel sonata.[4] The ground plan is the same; it is only certain modifications of detail, imposed by the medium, that need be explained.

It is universally agreed that it was Mozart who shaped the lines of the modern concerto, and the main features of his work may be summarized as follows:

(1) The concerto grosso disappears; concertos henceforward are normally written for a single soloist.

(2) This soloist is definitely a virtuoso—more and more so, indeed, as time goes on. Mozart, Beethoven, Brahms, Elgar, Rachmaninoff—few will deny that from a purely technical

---

[4] From this dictum one must except Bach's so-called organ sonatas. These are really trios for two manuals and a pedal, and their organization, so far as outline goes, is essentially that of the Bach concertos.

standpoint these names suggest an increasing order of difficulty in execution.

(3) The work is in three movements, of which the middle one is a slow movement, cast in one of the various forms enumerated on p. 31. The first movement is in first-movement form, the last is more often than not a rondo. (This holds good, generally speaking, throughout the classical period, and even beyond it. Brahms's Second Piano Concerto and Elgar's for the 'cello are in four movements, but they remain exceptions to this day.)

Mention was made above of certain modifications of detail necessitated by the nature of the concerto medium. About these it is obviously impossible to generalize. One cannot say before-hand which themes will be given to the solo and which to the tutti and which to both, or how the solo is likely to decorate a theme in order to present it effectively on his own particular instrument, or how the dialogues will be arranged. To say that these details vary in every given work is merely to say in other words that the concerto, like every other piece of music, is (or should be) a product of the creative imagination. There is, how-ever, one point of procedure that can be described in general terms, and that concerns the lay-out of the opening movement.

It will be recalled that normally in the symphonies and sonatas of Haydn and Mozart, and frequently in those of Beethoven and Brahms too, the exposition closes with a double bar and is then repeated. In the concerto the procedure is as follows:

First there is an abbreviated exposition by the tutti. Not all the thematic material is presented, and the tonic key prevails throughout, such modulation as occurs being only of a transitory and incidental nature.

Then the solo joins in and the exposition is repeated, this time with all the material, and the usual key distribution.

It is surprising how this method held its ground long after the practice of repeating the exposition in sonatas and symphonies had become the exception rather than the rule. Beethoven (in his G major Concerto) gave the opening bars to the solo by way of innovation, and in Brahms's B♭ Concerto, and again in his

Double Concerto in A minor for violin and 'cello, the soloists get an imposing preliminary flourish, but this does not amount to a modification of the essential structure. As soon as the preliminaries are over, the twofold exposition follows on the usual lines. The most noticeable exception to this procedure—among standard concertos of otherwise orthodox construction—is Mendelssohn's perennially fresh Violin Concerto, where the soloist enters at once with the main theme, and there is no first exposition by the tutti. This seems a perfectly logical and reasonable proceeding; if a double exposition is no longer felt to be essential to the symphony, why should it be so to the concerto? Nevertheless, Mendelssohn was here in a minority.

There are, of course, plenty of well-known nineteenth-century concertos which diverge in this as in other respects from traditional procedure. It could not be otherwise, for the Romantic period was in many ways a period of revolution. One has only to think of such names as Schumann, Liszt, Max Bruch, Tchaikovsky, in this connexion. But these works are all experimental in a greater or less degree. They make no pretence of being built on traditional lines, and might better be described, so far as their form is concerned, as fantasias for soloist and orchestra. And fantasias are wayward and individual growths; one cannot possibly make any general statement about the method of their construction.

One should perhaps say a few words about the cadenza. The cadenza, in concertos, is a brilliant passage for the soloist, as a rule unaccompanied, occurring normally near the end of the first and occasionally also the last movement. It was originally supposed to be an improvisation, but later composers preferred as a rule to write their own; and even in the earlier ones the cadenza actually played at a modern performance is almost certain to be one specially written beforehand. Few performers in these days would trust themselves to improvise a cadenza for one of the great classical concertos, and such mistrust is doubtless well grounded. Parry says of cadenzas in general: 'With regard to their form there is absolutely no rule at all. They should contain manifold allusions to the chief themes of the movement, and to be successful should be either brilliant or very ingenious.' In most of the classical concertos the cadenza was ushered in by a pause on the $^6_4$ chord; a shake by the soloist on the dominant announced that the cadenza had run its course, and gave the signal for the tutti to re-enter and bring the movement to a close. In this brief final tutti the soloist originally took no part, but after Mozart's time this rule was soon broken down. In modern concertos, of course, the cadenza is no longer such a stereotyped affair; the composer will introduce cadenzas or cadenza-like passages whenever he feels like it, and will not necessarily enjoin total silence on the part of the tutti during their performance. See, for example, the entry of the solo violin in the first movement of Brahms's Concerto, or the remarkable accompanied cadenza in the last movement of Elgar's for the same instrument. Also very felicitous is Mendelssohn's treatment of the cadenza in the first movement of his Violin Concerto; the cadenza—a shortish one— comes, not at the end of the recapitulation, but at the end of the development, and gradually subsides into a quiet across-the-strings arpeggio figure which is maintained unbroken while the tutti steal in pianissimo, almost unobserved, with the recapitulation of the opening theme. Nothing could be simpler, yet in the whole of musical literature it would be hard to find a happier touch of craftsmanship.

VIII

Variation Form. The Overture

1. *Variations*

There are many ways in which a theme may be varied, but we shall find, on examination, that most if not all of them may be grouped under two headings:

(1) Those in which the melodic outline of the theme is preserved in some way or other.

(2) Those in which the melodic outline is ignored, the variations taking the form of independent studies worked out on the structure and harmonic framework.

Each of these aspects of variation writing has tended in turn to predominate over the other at certain periods of musical history. In a sense, the origin of variation writing traces right back to the pre-instrumental polyphony of the fifteenth and sixteenth centuries. Many of the masses then written took the form of contrapuntal embroidery written round a plainsong or even a secular melody. In the earlier period this melody was sung in long notes, usually by the tenor, throughout each movement of the mass; the melodic intervals were preserved, but naturally the rhythm had to be adjusted according as a particular movement was in duple or triple time. In the golden age of this polyphony, the period associated especially with the name of Palestrina, this method was discarded; but the practice of making each movement of the mass introduce the melody from which it was named still continued, and slight variations in the original form of the melody were accepted as being legitimate and artistically desirable. Here, for example, are some of the forms taken by the melody in Palestrina's mass, *Aeterna Christi Munera*;[1] bar-lines

---

[1] Reproduced from the author's *Contrapuntal Technique in the Sixteenth Century* (exx. 195–195D).

have been inserted, not at regular intervals in accordance with
the time-signature, but so as to show the natural rhythmic flow
of the melody (cf. the example from Byrd on p. 90):

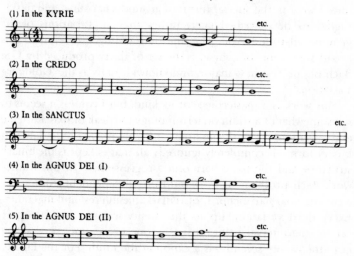

(1) In the KYRIE

(2) In the CREDO

(3) In the SANCTUS

(4) In the AGNUS DEI (I)

(5) In the AGNUS DEI (II)

But these early examples stand rather apart from variations as
we have come to understand the term. Variation writing proper
obviously pertains more to instrumental than to vocal music, and
it is in the work of our own virginal composers—Byrd, Bull,
Farnaby, and the rest—that the first specimens of genuine variation writing are found.

It must be admitted that these specimens are of more historic
than artistic value. The composers, with hardly an exception,
chose to ignore their tunes, which are often very charming. They
concentrated their attention on the harmonic framework, and
the variations they constructed on it consisted too often of
scale and arpeggio passages, now for one hand, now for the
other, in a progressively increasing order of rapidity, until the
climax comes in a whirling cascade of notes, whose musical
effect is certainly not commensurate with the difficulty of their
execution.

For the next hundred and fifty years or so variation writing

made little real progress. Composers continued to think more of
the bass than the tune (which after all is rather an important part
of the theme!), and the most successful specimens that were produced were in the special forms of ground, chaconne, and passacaglia (to be described later) rather than in variations of the
genuine all-round type. The one outstanding exception to this
broad statement, of course, is the set of thirty produced by J. S.
Bach on an Aria in G major, and known usually as the 'Goldberg
Variations'.

This work is a masterpiece of its kind, but I confess it seems to
me somewhat of a strain on terminology to speak of it as a 'theme
and variations'. The theme itself—a highly rococo little dance in
binary form—is completely ignored; all that is kept is the binary
structure and the basic harmonic progressions. On this framework Bach proceeds to work out thirty independent studies, for
a two-manual harpsichord, of remarkable interest and ingenuity.
Every third variation, up to the twenty-seventh, is a two-part
canon, the interval being raised by one every time, so that the
last—the twenty-seventh—is a canon at the ninth. For the Finale,
instead of the canon that was due, Bach substitutes a 'Quodlibet'
—a kind of contrapuntal pot-pourri of popular tunes—to bring
the set to a jovial conclusion, after which the tune itself is played
through once more in its original form, as though to remind
listeners how little it has had to say in the affair. 'Thirty-one
Fantasias on an Unfigured Bass' would have been a more
veracious description.

After Bach's death the pendulum swung the other way. In
Mozart's work, especially, the tune comes into rather more than
its own, and variation writing becomes almost entirely a decorative art, often very charming in effect, but lacking in structural
resource and intellectual content. Beethoven restored the balance;
but there is no need to carry beyond this point the purely historic
outline of evolution in the variation form. It will be of more use
now to describe in some detail the actual methods in which
a theme may be varied, and to quote some examples of each
kind.

(1) The tune may be kept in its original form, but transferred

to another part than the top one, with (necessarily) some alteration in the harmony and texture. See, for instance, the first and
third of Brahms's Pianoforte Variations on a Theme by Schumann
(op. 9); but the best example is perhaps the little set of variations
on the 'Emperor's Hymn' that forms the slow movement of
Haydn's C major Quartet (op. 76, No. 3). Here the tune is simply
passed from one instrument to the other in turn, the other instruments weaving a light contrapuntal texture around or above it.
For the Finale the tune is re-transferred back to the first violin,
with a new harmonization.

(2) The tune may be kept substantially in its original form and
position, but with increasingly rich and varied harmonies. Many
of the variations in Delius's *Appalachia* and *Brigg Fair* are thus
contrived.

(3) Palestrina's method of preserving the melodic outline but
altering the rhythmical conformation may be followed, e.g. in the
first section of the first of the 'Enigma' Variations, where this
phrase of the melody

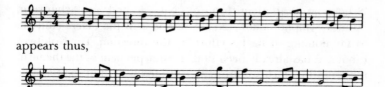

appears thus,

the basic harmonies being unchanged, but the texture greatly
elaborated.

(4) The essential melodic outline may be presented in a more
decorative guise. This is so common as scarcely to need illustration; the last variation in the opening movement of Beethoven's
Pianoforte Sonata in A♭ (op. 26) will serve as a case in point.

So much for the methods whereby the tune itself, or a complete section of it, may be preserved more or less intact in variation form. We have now to consider those in which it may be
broken up, and rhythmical units or characteristic figures made

to form the basis of the variations. First of all the contrapuntal possibilities may be reviewed.

(5) Without resorting to any special devices, characteristic fragments of the tune may be woven together into a freely contrapuntal movement in binary or ternary form. The happiest example I know is No. 5 of the variations in the last movement of Beethoven's E major Sonata (op. 109). Its gay incisiveness is in such contrast with the grave serenity of the theme as to be almost a parody, yet under the disguise the essential outlines of the latter are clearly discernible.

(6) Fugue, fughetta, or the more free fugato, on a subject taken from a prominent series of notes in the theme (usually the opening), are frequently met with, though a large-scale fugue is naturally kept as the climax of a long and elaborate set, such as Beethoven's 'Diabelli' variations or those by Brahms on Handel's theme (op. 24).

(7) Canonic treatment of thematic fragments is also not uncommon—see, for example, Brahms, 'Handel' Variations, No. 6; 'Schumann' Variations (op. 9), Nos. 8 and 14; Schumann, 'Études Symphoniques', No. 3 (Étude 4 in the Peters edition), to say nothing of Bach's efforts in this direction. The Goldberg canons, it has already been said, are independent of the theme in the sense in which we are now considering it; but the Canonic Variations on *Vom Himmel Hoch* for organ are based on the chorale itself (and behold, they are very dry).

(8) Double counterpoint and melodic inversion may also play their part. For the former see Brahms's 'Haydn' Variations (op. 56), No. 4, where the opening counterpoint of the oboes and violas is inverted at the twelfth in bar 11 by the upper woodwind and strings, the inversion corresponding to the repeat of the first half of the tune. For the latter turn to var. 8 of the same set and observe the take-up by the woodwind (in bar 6) of the opening string figure; in the second half the violin figure is similarly inverted four bars later by the violas.

[The thematic reference, by the way, is not an obvious one in either of these variations; the opening figure of var. 4 (oboe) and that of var. 8 (violas and 'celli) both relate to the first three bars of the theme, but both time and mode are changed, and in the second case there is also a certain amount of decoration.]

There remain two kinds of variation still to be considered, and those the most commonly used of all:

(9) Some one unit or rhythmical figure taken from the theme may be developed throughout the variation, the essential harmonies and bar structure of the theme being also more or less preserved. Examples of so common a method are hardly called for; but none the less I would invite the reader's attention to two very fine and very familiar specimens, to which reference has already been made—Beethoven's 'Diabelli' Variations (op. 120) and Brahms's set on a theme by Handel (op. 24). If he will bear in mind the melodic opening of their respective themes:

and then go through the variations observing the use that is made of the figures in square brackets, he will begin to see for himself what possibilities this method offers to composers who are not only men of genius but also complete masters of their craft (which many gifted composers are not).

(10) The same method of developing a single figure may also be employed with independent figures—with figures, that is to say, that have no relationship to any part of the theme. Examples of this method are to be met with here and there in most well-known compositions in variation form; the most extensive employment of it that I can recall is in the 'Études Symphoniques', where references to the melodic outline of the theme are few and far between.

It will occur to the reader at once that Schumann does not call this work simply 'Theme and Variations', but 'Symphonic Studies in Variation Form'. As a matter of fact there are countless other minor works—études, preludes, and the like—that are individually constructed in this manner, i.e. by taking some characteristic rhythm or figure, and working it through a definite scheme of harmonies and modulations. And in the same connexion one may well refer also to the modern type of lied, as exemplified by Schubert, Schumann, Brahms, Wolf, Fauré, and many others. In the great majority of their songs the accompaniment is based on a single definite figure, and it is this figure, rather than the vocal contour, which binds the whole together and gives it formal unity.

There is no generic name for these one-figure forms. If the figures are devised for some special technical purpose, as in the case of certain works by Chopin, Cramer, and others, they are usually called studies (or the equivalent of that in some other language). If the figures are employed as the accompaniment to a song, naturally they are welcomed into the large and somewhat promiscuous family known as 'Songs with pianoforte accompaniment'. Otherwise they may be called anything or nothing. In any case, it will now be apparent how closely they are related to the variation family—first cousins at any rate, and hardly once removed at that.

Just one more point. In (9) of the methods above described it is said that the essential harmonies and bar structure of the theme may be *more or less* preserved. Just how much more or how much less depends on the composer's fancy; obviously there must be a certain limit, a kind of gentleman's agreement, as it were, between the composer and his audience, if the connexion between theme and variation is to remain discernible.

Generally speaking, the great classical composers adhere pretty closely to the bar structure of their theme, but allow themselves a certain licence in the matter of the harmonic detail, especially in the later variations, when the main outlines of the theme have had time to impress themselves firmly on the listener's mind. Again the Brahms–Handel set are instructive from this point of view. The theme does not modulate at all; so clearly Brahms must allow himself a good deal of latitude if the variations are not to become unbearably monotonous. But he compensates this harmonic freedom in two ways—first, by adhering with unusual strictness to the eight-bar binary structure of the theme; second, by keeping certain of its melodic elements prominently in view, so that the thread of communication is never lost.

When a variation is based on some strongly marked and easily recognizable melodic or rhythmic figure taken from the theme, there is no need to be too conscientious about preserving details either of the harmony or the structure. The variation will easily be recognized for what it is—an independent study or train of thought, suggested in the first instance by some aspect of the theme, but allowed thereafter to shape its own course. Most felicitous examples of this are to be found in the 'Enigma' Variations—notably Nos. 2 (H.D.S-P), 6 (Ysobel), 7 (Troyte), and 9 (G.R.S.).

The special kinds of variation form known respectively as the ground, the passacaglia, and the chaconne can be briefly described.

The most general of these is the ground proper; this consists of a single phrase, never more than a few bars long, which is repeated over and over again in the bass, whilst new melodies and changes of texture are introduced in the upper parts. These changes need not necessarily coincide with the cadence of the ground; Purcell (with whom the form was a special favourite) is particularly adroit at concealing the 'joins' of the ground by making his melody move in irregular phrases across them. Occasionally the ground may be taken up into the upper or middle parts for a short time, for the sake of variety; but its normal place is in the bass—hence the name.

This form, as already stated, is a particular favourite with Purcell, and also with Buxtehude, but one need not search their works to find examples. The *Crucifixus* of the B minor Mass is universally known, and in more recent times the Finale of the Brahms–Haydn Variations is scarcely less familiar and (of its kind) scarcely less excellent.

The passacaglia only differs from the ground proper in that it was originally a dance, and that it is, strictly speaking, in slow triple time. The most famous example is probably Bach's monumental work for the organ in C minor (which, by the way, has been successfully orchestrated by Stokowski), while a very charming modern specimen is the passacaille from Ravel's Pianoforte Trio in A minor.

The chaconne, like the passacaglia, was originally a dance, also of a stately character, and also in triple time. It differs from it in that the ground is harmonized; the variations (or 'divisions') in a chaconne are not built on a monodic phrase, but on a series of chords. Once more Bach supplies the most obviously familiar example; but not less well known to us are Beethoven's Thirty-two Variations for Pianoforte in C minor, and the Finale of Brahms's E minor Symphony. These are chaconnes in all but name.

2. The Overture

Seeing that a prelude has no fixed form, one might well have expected to find that an overture has none either; for the two terms, if not absolutely synonymous, are to a very large extent interchangeable, so far as everyday usage goes. But in music it is otherwise. An overture is something as definite as a concerto or a sonata; moreover, like them, it was, up till 1750 or thereabouts, something very different from what it afterwards became.

The first operatic composer who took the overture seriously was Lully (1633–87), and the form he gave it was this:

(1) Short pompous introduction.

(2) Bustling allegro, freely contrapuntal in character, but too loosely put together to be described as a fugue.

(3) Lighter movement in binary form, often a minuet or jig.

The other name that is principally associated with the earliest form of operatic overture is Alessandro Scarlatti (1659–1725), the father of Domenico. He, working on parallel but independent lines, shaped his overtures thus:

(1) Lively allegro movement, usually of the canzona or freely fugal type.

(2) Short slow interlude.

(3) Binary movement of a dance-like character, similar to Lully's.

Not every overture by these composers corresponds in every detail to these standard patterns; that goes without saying. But the description may be taken as generally true. Historians are therefore justified in drawing a distinction between the French (or Lullian) and the Italian (or Scarlattian) type. But the distinction has been more emphasized than the case warrants. The most important elements, the contrapuntal allegro and the dance movement in binary form, are common to both; the difference only amounts to this, that in the French overture it is the first of these movements, in the Italian the second, that is preceded by a slow introduction.

Handel generally follows the French model, both in his operas and his oratorios. There are notable exceptions and modifications in the case of the latter. In *The Messiah*, and also in *Judas Maccabaeus*, the final dance movement is omitted, whilst in *Saul* the entire scheme is preceded by an extended allegro movement in free ternary form, so that the final result approximates more in scope to one of his concerti grossi, the more so, inasmuch as the fugal movement is freely interspersed with episodes for organ solo.

Bach's case is rather different. His great choral works—the masses, passions, and cantatas—have no fixed form of introduction, and his instrumental overtures (as he called them) are so extended in form as to resemble suites or partitas; that in B minor, in fact, for flute and strings, is almost always described as a suite. But if one examines them closely, one finds that they are in fact overtures, but with a group of dance-like movements at the end instead of the one (or occasionally two) with which Lully and his successors contented themselves. Also there is a slow movement both before and after the fugal allegro, so that altogether one has to strain a good many points to describe them as 'French' overtures. So far as they are 'overtures', they are in form just as much Italian as French. And as it would savour of preciosity to speak of Bach's 'Franco-Italian' overtures, the best course would seemingly be to call them simply 'overtures' and let the qualifying description go by the board.

By 1750, approximately, the type of overture we have been

considering had finally disappeared from the scene, together with the contemporaneous types of concerto and sonata. From that date onwards the overture was cast, as a rule, in something like first-movement form, with or without an introduction. It is often said that overture form is first-movement form with the development omitted, or conversely, that such a piece as the slow movement of Beethoven's D minor Sonata (op. 31, No. 2) is in 'overture form'. This is going rather too far. There are overtures, certainly, in which the briefest of links leads back from the end of the exposition direct to the recapitulation (e.g. Mozart's 'Figaro', Beethoven's 'Prometheus'); others, again, where the development is very short (e.g. 'Fidelio') or replaced by an episode based on a scene from the opera itself (e.g. 'Leonora', No. 1). But in the majority of the classical overtures cast in this form the development is of fair extent and importance. It does not approach the scale of the mighty developments in the 'Eroica' Symphony or the 'Hammerklavier' Sonata; but the same could be said of many other symphonies and sonatas. And perhaps it is just as well.

Since Wagner's time the full-dress operatic overture has tended to disappear. Modern opera prefers a short prelude or no prelude at all, and the overture has become frankly a concert piece, without necessarily ceasing to be cast in the old form. Brahms's 'Tragic' Overture is an example of such composition, and a truly magnificent one. The last of the really great operatic overtures was Wagner's 'Meistersinger'. This appears at a casual hearing to be cast on quite novel lines, but it is surprising to find, on analysis, how much it has in common with the old concerto form. There are various episodes, constructed from material that is to be used in the course of the opera; but the principal theme,

returns from time to time to dominate the scene, and binds the whole spacious framework together very much in the way of a Handelian ritornello.

PART II
THE CONTRAPUNTAL FORMS

IX

The Antecedents of Fugue

It was pointed out above (p. 17) that in the seventeenth century there was a confluence of two musical streams which had hitherto kept their courses apart. One of them—that of popular song and dance—has already been surveyed to some extent in Chapters I and III; the other—the music of the church tradition—has now to be considered. Logically, perhaps, this chapter ought to have been the second of the book, for (as we have seen) none of the 'harmonic' forms already discussed is independent of 'contrapuntal' influence, and it was impossible to give any detailed account of them without frequently anticipating the contents of this chapter. But this is merely to say, in effect, that the development of musical form cannot be set forth in a strictly chronological order, and it seems to me on the whole that this place, and not the earlier one, was most appropriate for these preliminary observations on fugue.

The sources of modern counterpoint are to be found in the church music of the sixteenth century, and that music is very different in style and idiom from music as we have known it for the last three hundred years. The scales are different, the harmony is different, the rhythm is different. Most students are vaguely aware that these differences exist, but there are many who, if asked, would be unable to define them with any degree of precision. A brief exposition, therefore, may not be out of place, for without some grasp of the style there can be no real comprehension of the form.

1. *Scale (or Mode)*

The modes employed were all formed from what we should call the white notes of the scale; that is to say, they were all diatonic, consisting of five tones and two semitones. Where they differed from one another was in the order of occurrence of these intervals; the following table enumerates them, together with the names by which they are traditionally known:

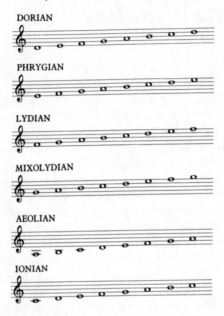

A further distinction was made according as the compass of any given melody lay mainly between the final (i.e. tonic) of the mode and its octave, or between the dominant and its octave. In the former case the mode was called 'authentic', in the latter 'plagal', the prefix 'hypo-' being used to distinguish the plagal from the authentic forms of the various modes. Thus, of the two following short melodies,

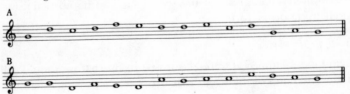

A, lying as it does between G and g, is in the Mixolydian mode, B, lying between D and d, in the Hypomixolydian (not the Dorian, because the finish is not on D, but on G). The distinction still exists, of course, in all tunes, though the terms have fallen into disuse; 'Blue Bell of Scotland', for instance, is authentic, 'Robin Adair' plagal.

In polyphonic compositions it was inevitable (owing to the natural compass of the different voices) that some parts should lie mainly within the 'authentic' and others mainly within the 'plagal' range of notes. In such cases the description of the composition as a whole was according to the compass of the principal tenor part. If his part was 'authentic', the whole composition was considered as being in an authentic mode; if plagal, plagal.

The only accidentals used were F♯, C♯, G♯, B♭, and E♭, and they were used principally for two purposes:

(1) melodically, to avoid the tritone or the false fifth;
(2) harmonically, to form what we should call a perfect cadence. In this position both chords were invariably major chords, the third being raised chromatically if necessary.

2. Harmony

This is not a text-book on harmony, and there is no occasion here for entering into any great detail. But it is important to remember that the whole harmonic structure of the sixteenth century rested on a foundation of consonance. Basically the only chords employed were the common chord and its first inversion. There is no such thing as what we should call an 'essential' seventh. It is quite true that dissonance was continually occurring, but *always*—apart from passing notes—in the form of suspensions, which had to be carefully prepared and as carefully resolved.

Modulation, in a restricted sense of the term, was constantly employed. It is evident that, by means of the accidentals enumerated in the last paragraph, cadences could be formed on various notes of any given mode, and modulation, in the sixteenth century, meant simply cadence, and nothing more. For us it means the temporary establishment of a new tonal centre, but such a conception as this would have been quite outside the purview of Palestrina and his contemporaries. It is perfectly correct to speak of 'modulation' as a feature of sixteenth-century music, but we must beware of reading into the term a wider significance than it could possibly have had at that time.

3. Rhythm

Even more different was the conception of rhythm. Rhythm to us suggests clear-cut phrasing, symmetrical balance, and strongly defined accentuation. To the sixteenth-century composers these things were anathema. It is quite true that their compositions were built on a metrical framework, in the sense that dissonance might only occur on certain beats of the bar.[1] But the rhythm imposed, so to speak, on this metrical framework was designedly irregular—a rhythm of prose rather than of verse. The accents were indicated at least as much by duration as by stress; they occurred in no sort of measured sequence; they did not even coincide in the different voices, each of which pursued its own untrammelled course. The following quotation from Byrd will serve to illustrate what is meant. In the first version regular·bar-lines are printed in accordance with the time-signature, and the words are omitted; it will be seen that the whole passage looks at first view like a perfectly uneventful bit of three-part counterpoint in common time. In the second version the words are added, and I have attempted to bar each part individually in accordance with the natural flow of the accents. The transformation is startling:

Byrd.—Who looks may leap (I)

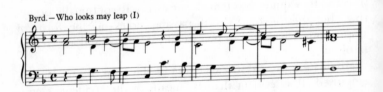

[1] 'Bar' is an anachronism, for the bar-line had not yet come into use. But the function of the modern bar is simply to rule off the music in strips of the length indicated by the time-signature, and it is both shorter and clearer to speak of 'bars' rather than 'metrical units' or something of the kind.

Idem (II)

(Who) speaks with heed, may bold-ly speak his mind.

(with) heed, may bold-ly speak his mind, may bold-ly speak his mind.

may bold-ly speak, may bold-ly speak his mind, speak his___ mind.

It is apparent that fugue written in accordance with these conventions of idiom and style is bound to be a very different affair from fugue in the Bachian and post-Bachian sense. It is sometimes argued that fugue is not a form at all, but a texture, and so far as the sixteenth century is concerned one may readily concur in this view. In the first place the subjects, being exclusively vocal and liturgical, are severely limited in character; they have neither the range, the mobility, nor the rhythmical individuality of true fugal subjects. They are not distinctive, they do not impress themselves on the memory. Furthermore the 'fugue' seldom or never gets beyond what we should call the expository stage; once the announcement of the subject in all voices is complete, there is frequently no further reference to it, either by development or repetition. If the composer wants to continue fugally, he simply starts another subject as soon as he is ready to begin a new sentence of his text. As an illustration of this procedure, I would cite Palestrina's four-part motet *Veni, sponsa Christi*,[2] which is really no more than a series of four fugal expositions, each of which is extended slightly by one or two 'redundant entries', as they would now be called. It would be absurd to call such a work 'formless', for the form in its way is very severe; but it is not the form of a fugue as we know it today.

None the less, the method of exposition here followed is very similar, as far as it goes, to that of classical fugue. The voices enter one by one with the subject; that has been accepted ever since as the correct procedure at the outset of a fugue. There may

[2] Quoted in full in the author's *Contrapuntal Technique in the Sixteenth Century* (ex. 192).

even be a counter-subject, invertible at the octave, or occasionally at the twelfth, with the principal subject: Marenzio, *Tradent enim*:

As regards the answer, it was supposed to be a 'real' (i.e. an exact) answer; if the answer was modified in any way, the fugue was considered merely as a 'fugue of imitation', not as a real fugue. The answer could be made, as we should put it, in the tonic, the dominant, or the subdominant; but once more I must remind readers that such terms, in this connexion, are anachronisms. The answer was actually determined by a process known as the 'solmization of the hexachord'—a formidable name for what was in reality quite a simple process, into whose details we need not enter here. (*Grove* will elucidate for those who are curious, s.v. 'Hexachord' and 'Solmization'.) The result in practice was, as I have said, that the answer could be made, in modern parlance, at the unison, octave, fourth, or fifth (above or below).

Of particular interest, sometimes, are the modified answers given in the 'fugues of imitation'. They are unsystematic, and show many curious vagaries; but they also show that in practice, if not in theory, the octave was beginning to displace the hexachord, and also that the octave was felt from the first as tending to divide at the fifth into two unequal overlapping halves:

so that a leap from tonic to dominant in the subject could appropriately be answered by the converse leap from dominant to tonic, and vice versa. This tendency, as we shall see in the next chapter, became a firmly established principle in classical fugue.

The next step in the historical evolution of fugue is provided by the instrumental 'fantasias' of the early seventeenth century, notably those of Byrd and Gibbons. It was quite natural that composers in the early stages of instrumental composition should seek first of all to adapt the existing vocal forms; one cannot solve every problem at once. And these early 'fantasias' do not differ in essential outline from the vocal 'fugues'—if one can call them so —that we have just been considering. They are slightly more mobile, perhaps, but the ground plan is still merely that of successive expositions loosely strung together. The rhythm is still the freely flowing rhythm of vocal counterpoint, and the key system rudimentary, being obviously in a state of transition between the old modal and the modern scalic systems. Yet without these primitive models it may be doubted whether the string fantasias of Henry Purcell,[3] composed some fifty years later, could ever have been written. Like their prototypes, they are built in sections; like them again, they proceed by a uniformly contrapuntal method which must at that time have seemed to point back to the past, not forward to the future. But the counterpoint is far bolder, and the resulting harmony incomparably richer, than anything Byrd or Gibbons could well have devised. The sections contrast mutually in pace and style; the subjects are genuinely instrumental in character and adequately worked out; the modulations, even today, are often startling. They are, in short, mature works of genius, and though their outline is still very different from that of a modern fugue, it is by the continuous employment of fugal texture that their effect is obtained.

A closely allied form—and another favourite of Purcell's—is the instrumental canzona. This must not be confused with the vocal canzona, which was a sixteenth-century form of composition, something akin to the madrigal. The instrumental canzona is the link between the older 'fantasias' and the fully developed

[3] Curwen's issue of these fine works, edited by the late Philip Heseltine ('Peter Warlock') and André Mangeot, is far too little known, and the works themselves far too little played by quartet parties.

fugue of Bach and his contemporaries; indeed, one might say that practically all the 'fugues' of the late seventeenth and early eighteenth centuries are canzonas, whether labelled as such by their composers or not. Bach only uses the term once, so far as I know—in the organ canzona in D minor (organ works, Peters edition, vol. iv, p. 58); and this differs from the Purcell canzonas in being in two clearly defined sections. Its real affinity is with the fugues of Buxtehude, which are similarly in sections (usually three), although Buxtehude calls them simply 'fugues', and not 'canzonas' or 'fantasias'. Evidently the terms were largely inter-changeable, and even today, if one were asked off-hand to define a canzona briefly without entering into technical details, one would probably say merely that it was a kind of free fugue. The points of difference may be summed up as follows:

(1) The key system in the exposition is not so strictly ordered.

(2) Such devices as stretto, inversion, the more artificial kinds of double counterpoint (all of which, by the way, were well known to Palestrina and his contemporaries) are not employed to any great extent.

(3) The thematic possibilities of the counter-subject are not explored.

(4) The episodes are not developed, after Bach's practice, from the subject and counter-subject; the composer is content to carry on the prevailing type of movement and general style until he is ready for his next entry.

All of these inventions and devices were in due course discovered or perfected, as the case may be, by J. S. Bach, who is the real creator of fugue as a form. It is to his work that we must now turn.

X

Fugue

Before considering the details of fugal construction, it seems advisable to say somewhat about the general outline of a fugue. It is commonly said that a fugue falls normally into three well-defined sections—the exposition, the development, and the final section. Some fugues do, but anyone who starts by assuming that these lines of demarcation are to be found in every fugue will find himself woefully entangled. A fugue (so called) may be definitely in binary form, just as a binary movement, without being labelled 'fugue', may nevertheless be one.[1] Book I,[2] No. 6 (D minor) and Book II, No. 21 (B♭ major) are as definitely binary as any movement in the suites. True, there is not actually a double bar; but the divisions at bar 21 of the D minor, and at bar 32 of the B♭, correspond precisely to the double bar of a courante or saraband, both in the resumption of the opening theme in the new key and in the repetition, at the close, of the half-way cadence. And there are many other fugues, not constructed quite on these lines, which it is nevertheless impossible to split up into three definite sections. Book I, No. 7 (E♭) proceeds to its final cadence without a break of any kind; so (to name no others) do No. 10 (E minor), No. 11 (F major), and No. 21 (B♭ major); Nos. 13 (F♯ major) and 18 (G♯ minor) have merely one final entry in the tonic by way of coda. Only the most Procrustean of analysts could look on these fugues as being in any real sense tripartite.

At the same time there are many fugues that do divide readily into three sections, both individual fugues like I. 4 (C♯ minor) and also certain definite types of fugue—double fugues, for

---

[1] See above, p. 9.
[2] Book I and Book II, throughout this chapter, refer, of course, to the two volumes of the 'Forty-Eight'.

example, such as II. 4 (C♯ minor); II. 14 (F♯ minor); II. 18 (G♯ minor); and the F major organ fugue that follows the well-known Toccata; also fugues with a recapitulation, such as I. 3 (C♯ major); II. 13 (F♯ major) and the Organ Fugue in E minor ('The Wedge'). We have already agreed (at least, I hope we have) that the terms 'binary' and 'ternary' have acquired, for musicians, a rather more restricted significance than their actual derivation would suggest. Not every composition in two sections is 'binary', nor every one in three 'ternary'. In accordance with this understanding, it will save confusion if the description 'binary' be reserved for fugues such as I. 6 and II. 21, and 'ternary' for such as I. 3 and II. 13, among those that have already been mentioned. Fugues *per se* are neither binary nor ternary in the conventional sense of those terms.

This clears the way for a more detailed inquiry into the normal method of fugal construction, and this inquiry falls most naturally into three divisions, viz.:

(1) the exposition;
(2) the development, or main body of the fugue, with special reference to the episodes;
(3) special devices, such as stretto, inversion, augmentation and diminution, and the more artificial forms of double counterpoint.

When these have been reviewed, there will still remain certain special types of fugue to be considered: double fugues, vocal fugues with an independent accompaniment, and fugues on a chorale. For the moment, let us confine our attention to 'straight' fugue, beginning with the exposition.

1. *The Exposition*

The exposition proper consists of successive announcements of the principal theme by each voice in turn. There is no fixed order of entry for the different voices, but if we take a typical scheme of entry from the top voice downwards, the lay-out of an absolutely strict four-part exposition will be somewhat as follows:

(1) Subject announced solo by the top voice (tonic key).
(2) Answer announced by the alto voice (dominant key);

counter-subject in top voice. This may be followed by an episode, or by a short codetta modulating back to the tonic key.

(3) Subject announced by tenor voice (tonic key); counter-subject in alto; free counterpoint in top voice. Possibly another codetta.

(4) Answer announced by the bass (dominant key); counter-subject in tenor; free counterpoint in the other two parts.

Various questions ask themselves at this point:

(1) Is the key order *invariably* tonic, dominant, tonic, dominant?

(2) What is a counter-subject?

(3) What is a codetta, and why?

(4) Is the answer merely the subject in another key?

Let us consider these points in succession:

(1) Tonic, dominant, tonic, dominant is the normal order; but occasionally one finds T, D, D, T (I. 1, C major), or T, D, T, T (I. 12, F minor; I. 14, F♯ minor). Very rarely the answer is made in the subdominant instead of the dominant (I. 18, G♯ minor; Beethoven, Quartet, op. 131, first movement; *Kunst der Fuge*, Contrapunctus X).

(2) The counter-subject, as its name implies, is a subsidiary subject that may accompany the principal subject either above or below. It follows that a subject and its counter-subject must make proper double counterpoint in two parts.

Contrary to theoretic rule, it is not essential that every fugue should have a regular counter-subject. Plenty of Bach's do not, especially those in which stretto, inversion, &c., present alternative features of interest; e.g., I. 1, C major; I. 20, A minor; II. 1, C major (the apparent counter-subject here is no more than a figure borrowed from the principal subject); II. 5, D major; II. 12, F minor.

Some, on the other hand, have two counter-subjects, which must then form triple counterpoint with the principal subject. That is to say, each theme must fit correctly either above, or below, or being the other two; e.g. I. 2, C minor; I. 4, C♯ minor (note that in this particular fugue neither counter-subject forms part of the exposition; the first is introduced at bar 36, the second at bar 49); I. 21, B♭ major; II. 17, A♭ major. One (I. 12, F minor) even has three, although the third of these only appears twice—in bars 14 and 15 (tenor) and bars 28 and 29 (alto). (I wonder, by the way, how many people noticed this before Tovey pointed it out; certainly I myself never did.)

(3) The exposition being in two alternating keys, it is some- times necessary to introduce brief modulating passages to estab- lish the proper key—tonic or dominant as the case may be—for the forthcoming entry. Such passages are known convention- ally as 'codettas', and where their function is purely tonal, the name will serve well enough. Where they are of sufficient length, and sufficiently definite in construction, they are, of course, neither more nor less than episodes, and there is no reason why they should not be called so. An episode's an episode for a' that, whether it comes in the course of the exposition or in the later stages of a fugue; see, for example, I. 12, F minor (bars 10–13); I. 14, F♯ minor (bars 11–15); II. 11, F major (bars 9–14).

(4) Fugue answers are classified as 'real' or 'tonal' according as they are or are not an exact repetition of the subject in the new key. To find out which kind of answer is the right one, it is best first of all to classify subjects as modulating or non-modulating. By a non-modulating subject, in this connexion, is meant a sub- ject that ends, as it began, in the tonic, no matter what modu- lations or chromaticisms it may have suggested *en route*. By a modulating subject is meant one that starts in the tonic and ends in the dominant. Let us consider the non-modulating subjects first.

The general rule is that such a subject takes a real answer. But if the subject starts on the dominant note, the answer starts on the tonic note; and if the subject starts with a leap from tonic to dominant (or vice versa), the answer will start with a converse leap from dominant to tonic (or vice versa). These modifications may entail some further slight modification, in order to restore the original conformation of the intervals found in the subject.

A few illustrations will make this plainer than any detailed explanation could:

(I. 3).
Subject:

Answer:

The subject starts on G♯ (the dominant); therefore the answer starts on C♯ (the tonic). The interval of a major second (G♯–A♯) at the opening of the subject has accordingly to be modified into a major third at the opening of the answer. I. 11, F major, and I. 16, G minor, are precisely similar. In II. 2, C minor, instead of a second becoming a third, a third becomes a second, and similarly in II. 24, B minor, and many others one could name. There is no need to quote further examples of this very simple procedure.

The next two show how leaps between tonic and dominant are modified in the answer; in the second of them, a further modification (in bar 2) is also necessitated:

(I. 13).
Subject:

Answer:

(II. 7).
Subject:

Answer:

It is not necessary that tonal answers of this kind should be harmonized from the outset in the dominant key. The whole

process is really based on the old distinction between the 'plagal'
and 'authentic' forms of the scale (see above, p. 88), and the
object of the modification is not primarily to reproduce the subject in the dominant key (which would not of itself entail any
modification), but to give its approximate equivalent in the corresponding plagal or authentic register. Sometimes the change of
key is made simultaneously (as in I. 13 quoted above); sometimes
the change is deferred until nearly the end of the answer, as in
I. 8:

while in one extreme case (I. 17, A♭), subject and answer are both
given entirely in the tonic key, and only in the ensuing codetta is
there a modulation (and that of the briefest) into the dominant.

In the case of modulating subjects, the traditional rule is that
the modulation from tonic to dominant in the subject requires
the converse modulation (from dominant back to tonic) in the
answer. To find the right answer one must therefore determine
the exact place in the subject at which the change of key is made
(implicitly or explicitly), and then regard the subject as being in
two sections. The tonic section is then reproduced by the answer
in the dominant, the dominant section in the tonic. Consider the
following:

Evidently one may regard the theme as being in the tonic up to
the first note A in bar 3, and in the dominant from that point on.
The G in bar 3, therefore, is not the supertonic of the key F; it is
the dominant note of the key of C (the dominant key), and must
therefore be answered by C, the dominant note of the key of F
(the tonic key):

One more to make it extra clear:

Here the changing place is self-evident. In bar 3, accordingly, the first F♯ is the mediant of D (the tonic key), and must be answered by C♯, the mediant of A (the dominant key). The second F♯ is the submediant of A (the dominant key), and must therefore be answered by B, the submediant of D (the tonic key):

In addition to this, it must be remembered that if the subject starts with a leap from tonic to dominant (or vice versa), precisely the same procedure takes place as in the case of non-modulating subjects:

(I. 7).

Subject:

Answer:

There are many modulating subjects which cannot be answered in accordance with the above rules without undue distortion. In such cases it is best to take the bull by the horns and give a real answer starting in the subdominant, as Bach does in I. 18:

Subject:

Answer:

Here the opening note G♯ (the·tonic) is naturally answered by D♯ (the dominant); apart from this (which is a pure formality and has nothing to do with the modulations), the answer is a real one.

Sometimes at the close of the exposition, before embarking on his middle section proper, the composer interpolates one or more extra entries of the subject in the tonic or dominant key. These are usually known as 'redundant' entries; II. 18, G♯ minor, has one such (middle voice, bar 19); II. 17, A♭ major, has three (starting respectively at bars 13, 16, and 22), before the first genuine 'middle entry' in the relative minor key comes at bar 24. Sometimes there is a complete set of such entries for every voice; this is known as a counter-exposition, and examples of it may be found in I. 1, C major; I. 9, E major; and I. 11, F major. In the counter-exposition the order of entry of the voices is usually different from that followed in the exposition proper, and the treatment is freer—e.g. the first entry in the counter-exposition need not be, and usually is not, a solo entry; the counter-subject (if there is one) may temporarily disappear, and so on.

2. *The Development*

Let us consider this part of a fugue, for the present, without reference to the special devices of stretto, inversion, &c., which will be discussed in the next section. These apart, it will be found that in the main body of a fugue there are two constituents:

　(1) the subject itself, which appears from time to time in its original form, somewhat in the manner of a ritornello;
　(2) the episodes which connect these recurrent appearances of the subject.

The first of these (which are known as 'middle entries') can be quickly dealt with. There is no rule as to their number; it depends on the length and general scope of the fugue. They confine themselves strictly, as a rule, to the circle of related keys: the D minor entry in the E minor fugue (I. 10) is an exception of a very rare kind. Be it noted, however, that the tonic itself is a member of the charmed circle. Anyone who may have obtained from text-books the idea that tonic (and even dominant) entries are never admitted between the end of the exposition and the beginning of the coda might first of all examine bars 36–94 of the great C♯ minor Fugue (I. 4). Incidentally he might count up and see how many bars of actual five-part writing he can find in these 60 or so bars of a five-part fugue, and remind himself at the same time that even three- and four-part fugues should not consist of exclusive and continuous three- and four-part writing. In other words, it is well to open a window occasionally and let a little air in.

These 'middle entries' may come singly or in pairs, or even larger groups, if the subject is a short one. If it is a long one, single entries are best, otherwise the fugue may be unduly protracted. They may take the form either of the subject or the answer (where these differ), and they may be accompanied always, or sometimes, or never, by the counter-subject. There is no fixed rule about it; but for a beginner in fugue one may safely say that 'always' or 'sometimes' is better advice than 'never'.

The episodes may consist of new material, or may be developments of ideas taken from the subject, counter-subject, or codetta.

Bach favours the latter, but has no hesitation about introducing fresh material when it suits his purpose. He is more inclined to do this in his organ fugues; see, for example, the fine episode (forty-eight bars long) that starts in bar 57 of the great C minor Fugue (the one that Elgar orchestrated), or that in the equally well-known one in the same key (Peters ed., vol. ii, p. 42), starting at bar 59 and continuing till bar 87—another unusually long episode.

Good specimens, however, may also be found in the '48'; see, for example, the episode that starts in the second half of bar 17 of the B minor Fugue (I. 24), and is repeated with slight variations in bars 26–30 and again in 65–9. Another instance (and a most amusing one) is to be found in I. 13, F♯ major, where the exposition is followed immediately by the introduction of a

seemingly insignificant little figure,

which is taken up at once by the other voices, and thenceforward is never out of the picture. It dominates the entire fugue, even the principal subject itself being quite overshadowed. Beethoven, as might have been expected, allows himself still greater freedom in these matters, and such episodes as that starting in bar 237 of the 'Hammerklavier' Fugue, or the return of the 'Arioso dolente' in that of the A♭ Sonata (op. 110), transform the texture and interrupt the normal continuity of the fugue to an extent that Bach probably would not have endorsed. But Beethoven's whole outlook on fugue, coloured as it was by his more turbulent and assertive personality, was very different from Bach's, and the fugues just quoted, to say nothing of the 'Grosse Fuge' for string quartet (op. 133), stand by themselves in fugal literature. A student who takes them or their like as models does so at his own risk, and must be prepared to meet the fate of Icarus.

Episodes that develop the subject-matter are more characteristic of Bach. The nature of the process known as 'development' has already been discussed in some detail (see p. 45), and it will suffice to say here that No. 7 of the methods there enumerated is the one most commonly employed in fugue, even as it is in sonata, symphony, and variations. A fugue whose subject and counter-subject do not contain easily recognizable units or rhythms that lend themselves to this kind of treatment is fore-doomed from the start—unless it be a stretto or other 'freak' type of fugue. Very few students succeed at first, and many of them never, in making their episodes absolutely definite and clear-cut, as Bach invariably does. In particular I would call their attention to

(a) the use he makes of sequence;
(b) the use he makes of dialogue between one voice and another;
(c) his habit of writing his episodes in double counterpoint, with or without a free part, so that a later episode is often

found, on examination, to be the inversion of an earlier one.

As regards (a), the passages I would suggest as worthy of specially close attention are:

I. 3, C♯ major, bars 31–5, and again 35–8, and again 39–41; I. 21, B♭ major, bars 17–22; II. 1, C major, bars 29–32 and again 33–9; II. 10, E minor, bars 17–20 and again 21–4; II. 11, F major, bars 61–5 and again 72–6. But it is scarcely possible to open these volumes without seeing a case in point.

As regards (b), I suggest particularly I. 16, G minor, especially the episode in bars 24–8, the dialogue in this case being between the two upper voices; I. 18, G♯ minor, bars 21–4 (dialogue between alto and bass); II. 1, C major (first episode, bars 13–19, repeated, in a slightly different form, bars 55–61); II. 6, D minor, bars 18–21, where all three voices participate in the dialogue on equal terms; II. 7, E♭ major, bars 45–53.

It should be observed that processes (a) and (b) are not so much alternative as complementary; sequence is frequently broken up into a dialogue, and dialogue tends to continue by sequence.

The inversion of episodes ((c) of the above) is also fairly common; e.g. I. 10, E minor, bars 15–18 (inverted in bars 34–7); II. 17, A♭, bars 11–13 (inverted in bars 14–16, and again, by means of triple counterpoint, in bars 19–21); II. 12, F minor, bars 17–22 (inverted in bars 33–8).

3. *Special Devices (Stretto; inversion, augmentation, diminution; double counterpoint of the more artificial kind)*

Stretto may be defined briefly as the overlapping, not necessarily at the same pitch, of two or more entries of the subject. If one voice starts to announce the subject, and another then does the same thing before the first one has finished, that, so far as it goes, is a stretto. Students frequently ask me whether, in that case, a stretto is not the same thing as a canon. The answer, of course, is that a stretto certainly *is* a canon, as far as it goes; but it seldom goes for more than a bar or two. One does not speak of a 'canon' unless the imitation continues for an entire passage or period—certainly for several bars.

One must contradict at the outset the idea, disseminated by certain academic teachers, that stretto is a normal feature in fugal construction, and that its proper place is towards the end of a fugue, so as to form a sort of architectural climax. It is no part of a composer's business to reject a good subject because it will not go in stretto, much less to force it into stretto, when it is reluctant, by mutilating the theme and distorting the harmony. Those fugues in the '48' in which stretto is prominent are I. 1, 4, 8, 20, 22; II. 5, 7, 9, 22. I do not say there are no others in which traces of a stretto are to be found; there are several. But those named above are the only ones in which stretto is made a prominent feature. And as for the notion that stretto is reserved as a climax for the final stages of the fugue, a brief glance at those here enumerated will serve to dispel the illusion. In I. 1 the first appearance of stretto is in bar 7; in I. 4 in bar 94; in I. 8 in bar 24; in I. 20 bar 27; in I. 22 bar 25; in II. 5 bar 14; in II. 7 bar 30; in II. 9 bar 10; in II. 22 bar 27—in every case except one at quite an early stage, having regard to the total length of the fugue.

Strettos do not necessarily involve more than two voices, nor include the entire subject. A stretto of the complete subject in all voices is exceedingly rare and difficult to construct. It is known as a stretto maestrale, and examples of it may be found in I. 1 (bars 16–19) and II. 5 (bars 44–7).

Inversion in the melodic sense should, of course, be distinguished carefully from the other kind of inversion—the inversion of harmonic intervals that we call double counterpoint. In thematic inversion each interval as it occurs in the subject is inverted melodically, so that, e.g.

(I. 6)

becomes

Not every theme makes sense when inverted, and one has to find out by a process of trial and error which is the best starting note for the inversion in any given case. Bach is very fond of the device; the *Kunst der Fuge* is perhaps the *locus classicus* for its employment, but he makes frequent use of it also in the '48'— e.g. I. 6 (22); I. 8 (64); I. 15 (20); II. 22 (42); the number in brackets denotes the bar at which the inversion first appears in its complete form.

Equally legitimate, though possibly less fertile, are the devices of augmentation (increasing the note-values) and diminution (reducing the note-values). For an example of the former see I. 8, E♭ minor, final section, starting at bar 62 (where incidentally, and again at bar 67, the augmented subject combines, in a curious kind of stretto, with itself in its original form). Another effective use of augmentation is the bass entry in bar 19 of II. 2, C minor; the fact that four-part harmony here appears for the first time in the fugue leads some authorities to consider the exposition as being in three parts only—a view that I should characterize as palpably erroneous, were it not for the fear of exciting controversy. For diminution see the little stretto-like exposition that starts on the last beat of bar 26 of II. 9 (E major). Another example that scarcely needs pointing out is the fugue of Beethoven's A♭ Sonata (op. 110), which employs inversion, augmentation, diminution, and even double diminution at one point or another; I refrain from giving exact references as students may prefer to do this little piece of excavation for themselves.

The inversion of subject and counter-subject at the tenth or twelfth (instead of the usual octave) is also a useful device for getting a certain novelty of effect without resorting to the invention of new material. For the benefit of readers who may not be familiar with these forms of inversion, a short appendix explaining the theory of double counterpoint (though without giving detailed rules for its practice) has been placed at the end of this chapter. Here, therefore, one need only refer to a few examples. Double counterpoint at the tenth is an exasperatingly difficult form of double counterpoint, and the only place in the '48' where it is employed is, to the best of my belief, in II. 16, G minor; see bars 45–8 (alto and bass parts) and again 59–62 (treble and tenor parts), and compare them with the original entry of subject and counter-subject in bars 5–8.

The same two subjects may be found inverted at the twelfth in bars 28–31 (treble and alto parts) and again (combining with the inversion at the tenth) in bars 59–62 (treble and bass), and again in bars 69–72 (alto and tenor). Only those who know by experience the mutually conflicting difficulties of these various forms of counterpoint can begin to appreciate the miraculous ingenuity—quite apart from the striking power and effectiveness—of this counter-subject. Other places that might be cited as examples of double counterpoint at the twelfth are: I. 2 (compare bars 5 and 6 with bars 17–18 and 18–19); II. 4 (compare bars 48, 49 with bars 55, 56); II. 23 (compare bars 27–9 with bars 42–4).

Note on the chief forms of double counterpoint

By far the commonest form of double counterpoint, it goes without saying, is double counterpoint at the octave. In this the upper part moves down an octave (or compound octave) or the lower part up an octave, or both. The following table shows what each interval becomes when thus inverted (it must be understood that the intervals in each case may be compound—i.e. a seventh may become a second (or a ninth or a sixteenth, &c.)):

$$
\begin{array}{cccccccc}
1 & 2 & 3 & 4 & 5 & 6 & 7 & 8 \\
8 & 7 & 6 & 5 & 4 & 3 & 2 & 1
\end{array}
$$

In double counterpoint at the tenth, the upper part moves down a tenth, or the lower part up a tenth (the other part may remain stationary, or move an octave in the opposite direction). Table of intervals:

$$
\begin{array}{cccccccc}
1 & 2 & 3 & 4 & 5 & 6 & 7 & 8 \\
3 & 2 & {8 \atop 1} & 7 & 6 & 5 & 4 & 3
\end{array}
$$

In double counterpoint at the twelfth, similarly, with 'twelfth' substituted for 'tenth' (in the example from Marenzio, quoted on p. 92, the movement is, exceptionally, at the fifth, not the twelfth;

but so far as the transformation of intervals goes, the result is the same).

Table:

1	2	3	4	5	6	7	8
5	4	3	2	8 ⎱	7	6	5
				1 ⎰			

It should be understood that in the more artificial forms of double counterpoint the chromatic alteration or modification of intervals (from major to minor, imperfect to perfect, &c.) is permitted if necessary to improve the harmonic sense. Thus, in the following:

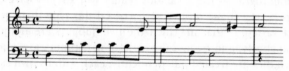

the raising of the two notes marked + in the inversion is perfectly legitimate, though in this case the strict equivalents (B♭ and C♮) would also be possible:

Bach avails himself freely of this licence; see, for example, the passages from I. 2 (bars 5–6 and 17–19) to which reference has already been made.

XI

Special Types of Fugue.
Canon, Round, and Catch.
Chorale Preludes

1. *Double Fugue*

A double fugue, as the sagacious reader will already have begun to suspect, is a fugue on two subjects. Of this type there are two distinct varieties—that in which the two subjects are announced simultaneously, and treated throughout in combination, and that in which they are treated independently, each with its own exposition (and possibly development as well), before being combined in the final section of the fugue.

The first of these does not differ greatly in construction from an ordinary fugue with a regular counter-subject, except that the exposition is rather more free. It is not necessary that each subject should be exposed in every voice. The function of the exposition in this case is to familiarize the listener with both subjects in tonic and dominant keys, and two combined entries may well be deemed sufficient for this purpose, provided that the second subject appears on top in one of them. The two subjects are not, as a rule, of absolutely equal length, the first having usually a bar or two by itself before the second joins in.

Examples of this kind are not hard to discover. Prout quotes choral examples in his *Fugal Analysis*, and the *Kyrie* from Mozart's Requiem Mass and 'Et vitam venturi saeculi' from the *Missa Solennis* are others that come readily to mind. For examples in instrumental music there are Handel's well-known keyboard fugues in G minor and B♭ major, and the great E♭ fugue that forms the climax of the 'Diabelli' Variations. It is not a favourite form with Bach, and there is no fugue of this type in the '48', but from his organ works one may cite those in B minor (Peters ed., vol. iv, p. 50), A minor (Peters ed., vol. iii, p. 85), and C minor (the Finale of the famous Passacaglia). In none of these, however, does he really appear at his best.

In the second type each subject in turn receives its own exposition and development (or possibly counter-exposition, as in Bach's organ fugue in C minor, Peters ed., vol. iv, p. 40), after which they are combined in various positions. This kind of fugue is Bach's own speciality; hardly anyone before him or since has employed it that I can think of.[1] Examples from the '48' are II. 4 (exposition of second subject starts at bar 35); II. 14 (exposition of second subject starts at bar 20) and II. 18 (exposition of second subject starts at bar 61). The second of these might more properly be called a triple fugue, as from bar 36 onward there is a concise treatment of yet a third subject (strangely like the first counter-subject of I. 4), which is then combined with the other two. Intermediate in kind is the well-known 'St. Anne' Fugue for organ. This has three sections and three subjects, but although the first is combined with each of the other two, the latter are not combined with one another. Call it, therefore, a double or a triple fugue, just as you prefer.

2. *Accompanied Fugue*

This, as the name applies, is a choral fugue in which the orchestra, instead of merely doubling the vocal parts, is given a role of its own to play. It is certainly a special *type* of fugue, but not, strictly speaking, a special *form*, for the general construction and lay-out of the voices (i.e. the purely fugal part of the affair) differs in no way from that of any other fugue. It is not, as a rule, the strictest kind of fugue, but there are plenty of unaccompanied or purely instrumental fugues of which the same could be said. Its particular problem is not one of construction, but one of instrumentation, and that is a subject with which we are not here and now

[1] The idea was known to Frescobaldi; see for instance No. 2 in Ricordi's Collection, *Fughe per clavicembalo . . . di antichi maestri italiani.* Bach was an insatiable student of other men's work, and may well have been acquainted with Frescobaldi's experiments.

concerned. One may perhaps, however, say this much on the subject—that the orchestral accompaniment is rarely *completely* independent of the voice parts, at any rate for any length of time. The subject is usually introduced over an independent bass, but as the other voices join in and the texture becomes more complicated, the tendency is for vocal and instrumental basses to support one another. And, generally speaking, it will be found that certain of the orchestral elements, at first glance independent, are really doubling one or more of the vocal parts in a more or less ornamental version.

It is not possible to formulate any set rules of procedure for such accompaniments. One can only recommend certain examples for consultation—notably the two famous fugues in Brahms's German Requiem ('For the righteous souls' and 'Worthy art Thou'), and (in a very different style) two of Mendelssohn's, namely the final chorus (*Preis sei dem Herrn*) from the 42nd Psalm, and the fourth number (*Denn sein ist das Meer*) from the 95th Psalm. Also to be included in this category is the opening section (exposition and counter-exposition) of what is perhaps the most remarkable fugue ever written—the opening chorus of Bach's cantata, *Es ist nichts gesundes in meinem Leibe*. Prout justly describes this masterpiece as a compendium of fugal composition;[2] it might equally well have been cited here as an example of double fugue, or of fugue on a chorale. As an example of independent accompaniment for strings to a strictly written vocal fugue, it is no less deserving of detailed study.

3. *Fugue on a Chorale*

Composition on a chorale has naturally a great deal in common with the older kind of composition on a canto fermo that was so extensively practised in the fifteenth and sixteenth centuries. Their idiom is rather different, but the method is essentially the same. It is not surprising, therefore, that the fugue on a chorale should closely resemble the old fugal motets of Palestrina and his contemporaries, as described on p. 91. Like

[2] *Fugal Analysis*, p. 35.

these, the fugue on a chorale consists essentially of a series of expositions the subjects of which are taken from the successive lines of the chorale. For a large-scale example of this method the best example is perhaps the opening chorus from Bach's Church Cantata *Ein' Feste Burg,* in which every line of that massive tune is made the basis of such a fugal section (not forgetting the repeats). A smaller and perhaps more readily accessible specimen of the same type is the organ fugue on 'Durch Adam's Fall' (Peters ed., vol. vi, p. 56).

In these two the chorale does not appear in its original form in combination with the fugue; but in many—most, indeed—it does so. As soon as the opening exposition has got under way, the first line of the chorale appears in long notes as an independent part, the fugue meanwhile continuing on its own course above or below (or both, if the tune comes in a middle part). As soon as the first line is finished the next exposition begins, and in due course the second line of the tune makes its appearance, and so on till the entire chorale has been thus worked through. The subjects of the various expositions, in such a case, usually appear as diminutions of that phrase of the tune which they respectively introduce.

For an illustration of this plan in Bach's choral works, there is the fugue on *Jesu Leiden* from the cantata 'Himmelskönig, sei willkommen'. I am not sure if this cantata is one of those published by Peters; but those who wish to examine this chorus and have not access to the Bach-Gesellschaft collection, will find it quoted in full in Prout's *Fugal Analysis* (p. 165). Once more, excellent examples are to be found in the organ works: *Ich hab' mein' Sach'* (Peters, vol. vi, p. 74), *Nun Danket* (vol. vii, p. 34), and *Wenn wir in höchsten Nothen sein* (vol. vii, p. 74).

It is also possible, instead of successive expositions, to have a continuous fugue on a single subject (either an independent subject or one formed from the opening notes of the tune), with the lines of the chorale appearing one by one, as before, in long notes above it, or below it, or in the midst of it. See, for example, *Nun komm' der Heiden Heiland* (vol. vii, p. 42), or the elaborately academic triptych, *Kyrie, Gott Vater, Christe aller Welt Trost,* and

Kyrie Gott heiliger Geist (vol. vii, pp. 18–25). Bach has given these a somewhat archaic flavour by arranging his canto fermo in semibreves throughout, and also by writing his expositions in close order (i.e. in a stretto-like formation), which was the normal sixteenth-century practice. They are not among the most appealing of his compositions for the organ, but they are of much technical interest, the last one especially (a four-part fugue for the manuals, with a chorale as an independent pedal part) being quite a *tour de force* of its kind.

4. *Canon*

Canon consists in the exact imitation, interval by interval, of one part by another. As a musical device, therefore, it is closely akin to fugue; indeed, the very name 'canon' is merely an abbreviation for 'fuga per canonem' (fugue according to rule), which was its original designation.

There are certain technical terms relating to canon which ought to be defined before we go any further:

(1) The voice or part which begins the canon is known traditionally as the *dux* or *vox antecedens*; the part which imitates it as the *comes* or *vox consequens*. 'Leader' and 'follower' are the simplest English equivalents.

(2) The imitation need not be at the octave or unison; it may take place at any interval above or below, and the description 'canon at the second (third, &c.), above (or below)' is the proper way to indicate this interval.

(3) Similarly with distance: the imitation may begin one bar, or one half-bar, or some larger number of bars or half-bars after the leader has started, so that we have to amplify the description further, 'canon at such and such an interval above or below at so many bars distance'.

(4) If two voices are taking part in a canon, it is spoken of as a canon two in one; if three, three in one, and so on. Sometimes (e.g. in the 'Dance for the Followers of Night', in Purcell's *Fairy Queen*) there are two simultaneous canons for two pairs of voices; this is known as a canon four in two, and similarly with any higher numbers; in the formula 'Canon X in Y', X refers

to the total number of voices engaged in the canons, Y to the number of canons that are going on simultaneously. (Byrd's *Diliges Dominum* is actually a canon eight in four, with the additional trifling complication that it may be equally well read from the end backwards, each follower being the exact reversal of its leader—a musical jigsaw of almost incredible ingenuity.)

Therefore, to characterize any given canon accurately and in full, one must speak of 'a canon so many in so many, at so many bars distance, at such and such an interval above or below'. This method of description holds good irrespective of whether there are or are not other free parts accompanying the canon.

Canons may likewise proceed by inversion (as in the twelfth and fifteenth of the 'Goldberg' Variations), or by augmentation and diminution. One of the movements in No. 6 of Purcell's *Sonatas of Three Parts* is actually a canon three in one by augmentation and double augmentation at the fifth and octave above, starting thus:

Obviously when two parts start at or nearly at the same time, and proceed canonically by augmentation, the part with the shorter notes will be complete, so far as the canon is concerned, by the time the other part has got about half-way. It then becomes a free part; so that although this form of composition may present difficulties up to that point, it becomes a very soft thing for the composer once that point is safely past.

It is perfectly possible to construct a canon *ad infinitum*, i.e. one in which each part is ultimately led back, by a double bar and repeat, to its own starting-point. Ouseley gives a simple instance in *Grove's Dictionary* (article 'Canon'). But as no two people desire to spend all their days in singing or playing the same canon over and over again, only to find their life's work still unfinished when Death intervenes, it seems rather a pointless amusement. Canons normally become free for a beat or two before the cadence that rounds them off; or, if they are introduced incidentally in the course of a longer composition, they are simply discontinued when the composer has had enough of them. One often finds brief canonic episodes of this kind interposed with happy effect; familiar examples are those in Beethoven's Fourth Symphony (first movement), Mozart's 'Prague' Symphony (slow movement), and Bach's C minor Prelude (I. 2). This is really the best way to treat canon; it savours more of mathematics than of music when it is taken too seriously, and even its disciplinary value can easily be over-estimated.

The round is merely a special form of canon at the unison for equal voices, in which each voice in turn, after completing its part, goes back to the beginning and repeats, until the last voice to enter has also had time to sing the complete part, after which a simple cadence brings the whole to a conclusion. The parts are generally printed vertically above one another in score, it being understood that as soon as the leader reaches the end of the first line, he goes on at once to the second, the next man in at the same time taking up the first line, and so on.

There is no theoretical reason why a round should not equally well be for mixed voices; but there is this practical difficulty—that owing to the different register of male and female voices, each part would have to make true harmony whether sung above or below the others. In other words, the round would have to be written in multiple counterpoint. This would not be necessary, however, if the round had an independent accompaniment to supply the true bass. The vast majority of rounds are unaccompanied, but there is one very famous example of a round with partly independent accompaniment—the quartet 'Mir ist so wunderbar' from *Fidelio*. In this case the canon is discontinued after the last voice to enter (Giacchino) has sung the first line, so that the multiple counterpoint is not fully tested; but it will be seen from the following score, that with an accompaniment worked on some such figured bass as I have indicated, any or all of the voices could interchange octaves without any infringement of the harmonic sense:

The catch is merely a round with punning words—'words' (to quote the description in *Grove's Dictionary*) 'so constructed that it was possible, either by mispronunciation or the interweaving of the words and phrases given to the different voices, to produce the most ludicrous and comical effects'. Both rounds and catches had an extraordinary vogue in England during the seventeenth and eighteenth centuries. Two of the most famous collections were *Pammelia* and its sequel *Deuteromelia*, published in 1609 by Thomas Ravenscroft (him of the Psalter).[3] Of later collections that of Warren, published in periodical instalments between the years 1763 and 1794, seems to have been the most extensive. The words, I regret to say, are often of a licentious character; Barclay Squire complains that many of Warren's are 'disfigured by obscenity of so gross a nature as to make them now utterly unfit for performance', and Tovey has observed the same peculiarity of some of Mozart's (*Ency. Brit.,* 'Contrapuntal Forms').

5. *The Chorale Prelude*

The form of any chorale prelude depends, in a sense, on that of the particular chorale on which it is composed, for the chorale itself is practically always[4] present, plain or decorated, in the prelude. One must therefore begin by saying, even though it is possibly superfluous, that the chorale is simply an old German hymn tune, composed or adapted for use in the services of the German Reformed Church after Luther's breach with Rome in 1520. As we know them now, these chorale melodies do not differ in technical construction from any ordinary English hymn tune. They are, none the less, of considerable antiquity, and many of them when they first appeared were cast in a somewhat different melodic and rhythmic mould from that in which they are now familiar. That, however, is by the way, and need not here concern us; those who are interested in the subject will find all the information they need in a little volume by Dr. A. W. Wilson,

---

[3] *The Whole Booke of Psalms: with the Hymnes Evangelicall and Spirituall. Composed into four Parts by Sundry Authors with severall Tunes.*

[4] See Harvey Grace, *The Organ Works of Bach,* pp. 269, 270, for the analysis of one or two exceptions.

entitled *The Chorales: their Origin and Influence* (Faith Press, No. 1 of 'Church Music Monographs').

In describing the chorale prelude, therefore, one is concerned, not actually with an outline, but with the possible methods of treating the tune which provides that outline. And in this case, instead of reviewing the subject chronologically, I propose to begin with a summary of Bach's own work in this direction and afterwards to say a few words about that of his predecessors in the field.

In spite of the great diversity of style and range displayed in Bach's chorale preludes, taken as a whole, the actual methods of treatment they exemplify may be quite shortly and simply summarized:

(1) Many of them are simply fugues on a chorale, which have been described earlier in this chapter.

(2) Many of them take the chorale tune just as it stands, and simply add to it parts of a more or less elaborate contrapuntal nature.

(3) In others the tune itself is elaborated, and the underlying parts, though still by no means devoid of independent contrapuntal interest, are concerned largely with giving appropriate harmonic support to the melodic embroidery.

Of (1) we need say no more, but (2) and (3) both require amplification.

As to (2), the first thing to note is that this type varies greatly in length, not only according to the length of the tune itself, but according to the way in which it is introduced. In the shorter preludes—those in vol. v[5]—the lines of the chorale are introduced successively with no break in between. In the longer ones the accompanying counterpoint is continued independently between the lines, and frequently there is quite a long stretch of it between the end of one line and the beginning of the next. Two settings of *Wer nun den lieben Gott lässt walten* will serve to show what a difference this may make. In V, p. 57, where there are no breaks,

---

[5] Throughout this discussion reference is to the collected edition of Bach's Organ Works published by Peters. Vols. v, vi, and vii are devoted to the chorale preludes, the longer ones being contained in the last two of these.

the prelude, including the repeat, is fifteen bars long. In VI, p. 76, where breaks occur, the length, with repeat, is forty-nine bars.

The other feature that is to be noticed—and that gives these preludes their characteristic interest and distinction—is the nature of the accompanying counterpoint. Occasionally—very occasionally—Bach is content to provide what is really no more than an elaborate four-part harmonization, as in V, p. 39 (*Liebster Jesu*). But almost invariably the counterpoint is based on some definite figure that persists imitatively throughout the prelude, adapting itself with the most uncanny skill to the harmonic requirements of the tune. Sometimes this figure is distributed amongst all the accompanying parts; sometimes it is limited to the middle voices, whilst the pedal part has an independent figure of its own; sometimes the tune will be treated in canon, with one voice, while figured counterpoint of some kind is maintained among the others. Bach's resources seem endlessly rich and inexhaustibly varied. I assume that readers who want to know (if they do not know already) what chorale prelude is, will obtain access to the Peters or to some other edition and study these wonderful works for themselves; if they do not, they will miss what is best in Bach. But in the meantime it can do no harm to print a few bars of some typical specimens, just to give a bird's-eye view of this method of contrapuntal figuration:

Alle Menschen müssen sterben

Vater unser im Himmelreich

We are considering these figures from a purely formal point of view, as so many patterns that are employed to give aesthetic unity to a musical design. But it goes without saying that they have also a profoundly expressive value, many of them being used with a definitely symbolic intent. This aspect of Bach's work is fully discussed by Schweitzer (*J. S. Bach*, chapters xxi–xxiii);

readers may also be referred to Harvey Grace (op. cit., pp. 114–23) for a concise exposition of the subject.

The third kind of chorale prelude, that in which the tune itself is embellished and decorated, neither requires nor is capable of any elaborate description. By this method Bach produced some of the most inspired and most deeply moving music of all time, but the method itself consists, as has already been said, simply in filling in the outline of the melody, and providing a suitably expressive set of harmonies, woven into a flowing contrapuntal texture. In a general way, there is really nothing more one can say about it. The melodic elaboration may be of varying degrees, the contrapuntal pattern may be more intricate or less, but the method remains fundamentally the same, alike in its more simple and its more complex application.

As an example of the less elaborate, I would quote the first two lines of *Herzlich thut mich* (vol. v, p. 30). The second is, in the original melody, just a repetition of the first:

In this prelude, it will be noticed, the repeat is represented by a higher degree of elaboration, both of melody and harmony, as compared with the first, but without losing its essentially direct and simple character:

At the other extreme is *Nun Komm', der Heiden Heiland* (vol. vii, p. 38). The first line of the tune runs thus:

while here is the corresponding place in the prelude:

Here, it will be seen, Bach has really gone far beyond the process of decorating and filling in the original melodic outline. He has extended and developed it according to the dictates of his fancy, taking the opening phrase of the tune, not as a complete thing-in-itself, but as an unfulfilled suggestion, an incipient curve, as it were, whose full course has yet to be traced. The other lines of the tune are treated in the same arabesque manner, and the whole is perhaps the most perfect of all Bach's examples of this instrumental coloratura.

The various forms of the chorale prelude are so intimately associated with the name of Bach, that one is tempted, almost unconsciously, to think of them as being his direct invention. That would be an error; so far as formal outlines were concerned, Bach had less actual invention to do in the case of the chorale prelude than in that of the fugue. The three principal types—the decorative, the figurative, and the fugal—were all in existence before Bach appeared on the scene. There is no need for anyone to take this statement on trust or alternatively to make elaborate researches in order to verify it. Dr. Straube (organist in the direct line of succession at the Thomaskirche in Leipzig) has made a most interesting collection of preludes of the pre-Bach era. This collection is published by Peters (3048), and contains representative specimens of all the great seventeenth-century German organists, from old Samuel Scheidt, who ante-dated Bach by almost exactly a century, down to such late contemporaries as Vogler and Krebs, both of whom outlived him. The former of these is represented by the curiously Bach-like *Jesu Leiden, Pein, und Tod,* which is actually included in the Peters edition (vol. ix) in the list of 'possibles', though there is no mention of it in the Bach-Gesellschaft edition. In a sense it out-Bachs Bach, for one or two of the arabesque figures contain such a multitude of very small notes as to be virtually unplay-able except in a tempo which, if adhered to throughout, would make other passages sound ridiculous. None the less it is a thing of real beauty, and could only have been written by one who had penetrated deeply into the spirit, and not merely followed the technical methods, of his great exemplar.

This one prelude apart, the collection is very different from any representative collection of Bach's own works; yet the difference, as I have already said, is not in the form itself, but in what Bach put into it. His resources, both in harmony and counterpoint, were incomparably richer and more varied than those of all his predecessors put together; alike in technical command and spiritual power he surpassed them in this field as greatly as he did Vivaldi and Corelli in theirs.

Yet what would he have achieved, had they not first shown him the way? One cannot answer that question, but one should not forget to ask it.

Appendix

ON VOCAL FORMS, AND THE SYMPHONIC POEM

People often speak casually of 'vocal forms' of music, and some may ask why there is no section of this volume devoted to their special consideration.

The answer—as will already be apparent to readers who have persevered thus far—is that the classification of music into 'vocal' and 'instrumental' forms is an illusory one, and that even if it were real, it would cut right across the method of classification I have followed. The form of vocal music must depend to a large extent, in any given case, on the particular words that have been chosen for setting, and to that extent elude any possible general-ization.[1] So far as it is independent of the words, so far, that is to say, as it depends on purely musical methods and principles of organization, it will be found to exemplify one of the various forms of instrumental music. We have seen already, in Chapter II, that the most vital elements of musical design—unity of time, unity of key, balance of phrase, repetition of pattern—were fully realized by composers of vocal music long before there was any instrumental music to speak of. Whether the first composers of instrumental music borrowed them deliberately from the pre-existent vocal music, or whether they discovered them inde-pendently by virtue of their inherent artistic fitness and serviceability, is no matter; the same conclusion follows from either premise, viz. that the fundamental principles of musical organization hold good, whatever the medium may be.

Consider the matter in rather more detail. All the contrapuntal

---

[1] The system of 'leit-motifs', in Wagner's later operas for example, is no exception, for these thematic sign-posts are not introduced in accordance with any uniformity of plan, but in order to throw light on what is happening on the stage at any given moment. In a sense they define the 'form' of an opera, but each form is individual and depends ultimately on the dramatic argument.

forms described in the latter part of this book are just as much vocal as instrumental; in fact, they were vocal long before they were instrumental. Canon, fugue, round—these are all older than instrumental music is, and to this day they are just as well suited to the one medium as the other. Nor is the chorale prelude necessarily a purely instrumental form; there are some of Bach's, including such familiar examples as *Wachet Auf* and *Ach bleib' bei uns,* which he transcribed himself from his cantatas.

On the other hand, the supposedly vocal 'aria form' (also anglicized into 'song form' and teutonized into 'lied form'), so far as it is a form at all, is not necessarily or exclusively a vocal one. The primary suggestion of the term, no doubt, is of that inevitable Da capo which held up the progress of every opera and aroused Gluck's especial and particular fury. But, outside the opera, there are hosts of arias that are not cast in this ternary mould. Many of them display, in a somewhat more elaborate form, some one of the binary patterns enumerated on p. 7; many others shape themselves freely to the verbal text without conforming to any formal pattern of the A B A C description. And in such cases, what really supplies the formal unity of the movement is the instrumental ritornello, which fulfilled this important function in vocal music long before it was appropriated for the same purpose by the concerto.

Take now a particular example—the Mass. The text of this does not vary from one generation to another, so that here, if anywhere, one might expect to find something that might properly be called a 'form' of composition. Yet in fact it is nothing of the kind. The text resolves itself first of all into the several sections of Kyrie, Gloria, Credo, Sanctus, Benedictus, and Agnus Dei, and these, ever since the Mass ceased to be a piece of pure vocal polyphony for liturgical use, have often been further subdivided into smaller component sections, such as the Gratias agimus, Quoniam tu solus, Incarnatus, Crucifixus, and so forth. But what further generalization can one make? How can one tell beforehand, in any given case, which sections are going to be set for chorus, and which for solo voices, singly or in combination? And even if one could, one would still be quite unable to say which of the choruses would be fugal and which antiphonal, which of the arias binary and which ternary and so on.

No. The history of the Mass is of very great interest; so is that of the Passion music, that of the opera, the oratorio, the cantata, and other branches of vocal composition. But none of them is a history of musical form in the sense in which we have been concerned with it in this volume. *Grove's Dictionary* and the general histories of music are the sources to which they should turn who are interested in such studies. To incorporate even the substance of them in these pages would swell the dimensions of the book far beyond its prescribed limit, and would, moreover, be irrelevant to the purpose I have tried to keep in view. Even the Madrigal and the Motet cannot find a place, for these again exhibit no uniformity of structure, unless they happen to be specimens of the fugal type described on p. 91.

For similar reasons one cannot explain, in any general terms, the construction of a symphonic poem. True, its medium is instrumental and not vocal, but its function is to portray in music a series of events or experiences described in or founded on some poem, legend, or narrative. Every symphonic poem, in short, has an argument, and its form as a whole is necessarily conditioned by that argument to a very large extent. As with purely vocal works, so here also one finds that many symphonic poems contrive, without losing sight of their argument, to get themselves cast into fairly regular instrumental shape. Don Quixote's adventures are portrayed in variation form, Till Eulenspiegel's— we have Strauss's word for it—in that of the rondo. So might Balakireff's *Tamar* appropriately have been; actually, following the outline of the poem, it is cast in a freely enlarged ternary form, of which it is an extremely fine specimen. Dukas's *l'Apprenti Sorcier,* likewise, agreeably to its argument, is in ternary form. Sibelius's *Tapiola* is developed with intense concentration from short rhythmic figures—almost too intense, indeed, for though *Tapiola* is a most vivid and powerful piece of music, one feels at times that the reiteration of a single note pattern is ceasing to be impressive and beginning to be wearisome.

I do not for a moment mean to suggest that symphonic poems

which do not happen to follow a more or less orthodox formal outline are therefore necessarily deficient or unsatisfactory in form; far from it. There are plenty of fine works in music, both symphonic poems and otherwise, which do not lend themselves to formal analysis on any of the stereotyped lines. All I mean is that a symphonic poem as such has no prescribed form. If anyone asks 'What is a symphonic poem?' the only general answer one can give is that it is a composition which seeks to portray, by purely musical means, a train of literary or pictorial ideas. One could not amplify this except with reference to individual cases.

Index of Names

[N.B. All references to specific works or writings of any individual are included in this index, even when the author's actual name is not mentioned in the text. The reference to *Peer Gynt*, for example, on page 26, is indexed under Grieg.]

Bach, C. P. E., 39
Bach, J. S., viii, ix, 18 (*note*), 20, 23, 27, 28, 29–31 (*passim*), 63–8 (*passim*), 70, 76, 78, 82, 83, 94, 95–109 (*passim*), 110–14 (*passim*), 119–24 (*passim*), 126
Balakireff, 127
Beethoven, ix, 7, 10, 11, 12–14 (*passim*), 24, 25, 28, 33 (*notes 2 and 3*), 35–8 (*passim*), 41–54 (*passim*), 55, 59, 60, 61, 70, 71, 76, 78, 79, 82, 84, 97, 104, 107, 116
Berlioz, 38
Bizet, 26
Brahms, viii, 35, 38, 43, 45, 47, 48, 49, 51, 53, 61, 70, 71, 73, 77, 78, 79, 80, 81, 84, 112
Bruch, 72
Bull, 75
Buxtehude, 81, 94
Byrd, 75, 90, 93, 115

Carroll, Lewis, 24
Chopin, 21, 80
Corelli, 28, 29, 63 (*note*), 124
Couperin, 18, 58
Cramer, 80

Debussy, viii, 38, 47
Delius, viii, 77
d'Indy, 38
Dukas, 127
Dvořák, 34, 38

Elgar, 8, 38, 64, 70, 71, 73, 77, 81, 103

Farnaby, 75
Fauré, 80
Franck, 38
Frescobaldi, 111 (*note*)

Gibbons, 93
Gluck, 126
Grace, Harvey, 118 (*note*), 122
Grieg, 26

Hadow, W. H., 8, 24, 35 (*note*), 44 (*note*), 51, 59, 62
Handel, 18, 27, 64, 68–70 (*passim*), 80, 110
Haydn, 12, 24, 27, 30 (*and note*), 33 (*note*), 35, 36, 39, 43 (*note*), 44, 54, 55, 71, 77
Heseltine, Philip, 93 (*note*)

Krebs, 124

Lambert, Constant, 57
Liszt, viii, 38, 72
Locatelli, 30
Lully, 82, 83

Mangeot, André, 93 (*note*)
Marenzio, 92, 108
Mendelssohn, 35, 72, 73, 112
Morley, 22
Morris, R. O., 74 (*note*), 91 (*note*)
Mozart, 20, 25, 27, 33, 35, 36, 43, 44, 52, 54, 55, 60, 61, 70, 71, 73, 76, 84, 110, 116, 118

Ouseley, F. A. G., 115

Palestrina, 74, 77, 90, 91
Parry, C. H. H., 10, 16, 19, 23, 72
Prout, E., 110, 112, 113
Purcell, viii, 21, 22, 28, 81, 93, 114, 115

Rachmaninoff, 70
Ravel, 26, 82
Ravenscroft, 118
Raymar, Aubyn, 61 (*and note*), 62
Rimsky-Korsakoff, 26

Scarlatti, A., 82
Scarlatti, D., 29, 39
Scheidt, 124
Schubert, 80
Schumann, 8, 34, 52, 72, 77, 78
Schweitzer, A., 121
Sharp, Cecil, 4, 6, 7
Sibelius, 36, 57, 127

Squire, W. B., 118
Stokowski, 82
Straube, K., 123
Strauss, R., 127
Streatfield, R. A., 68

Tartini, 29
Tchaikovsky, 72
Tovey, D. F., 8, 30 (*note*), 64, 98, 118

Vaughan Williams, viii, 26, 38, 64
Viadana, 63
Vivaldi, 64, 124
Vogler, 124

Wagner, vii, 78, 117 (*note*)
Warlock, Peter, *see* Heseltine
Warren, 118
Wilson, A. W., 119
Wolf, 80

Subject-Index

Allemande, 18, 19
Answer (fugal), 92, 96–102
Aria form, 126
Augmentation, 107, 115
Authentic modes, 88, 100

Binary form, 8, 23, 24, 33, 95
— in Domenico Scarlatti, 39–40
Bourrée, 20
Bridge, *see* Transition

Cadence, 6, 10–11
Cadenza, 72–3
Canon, 105–6, 114–16
Cantata, 16, 127
Canzona, 93–4
Cassation, 25
Catch, 118
Chaconne, 82
Chorale, 118–19
Chorale prelude, 118–24
Coda, 54
Codetta, 97, 98
Concertino, 63
Concerto, older form of, 63–70
— later form of, 70–3
Concerto Grosso, 65
— the Handelian, 68–70
Counter-exposition, 102
Counter-subject, 92, 97
Courante, 18, 19
Cyclic themes, 37–8

Development, methods of thematic, 45–51
Development Section, structural function of, 55
— in fugue, 102–5
Diminution, 107
Divertimento, 25
Double counterpoint, 49, 78, 96, 108, 109

Doubles, 20

Episodes, of a rondo, 58–61
— of a fugue, 102–5
Étude, 78
Exposition:
    in first-movement form, 40–4
    in a concerto, 71–2
    in early fugue, 91
    in later fugue, 96–102
    in double fugue, 110, 111
    in fugue on a chorale, 113–14

Fantasia, viii, 93, 94
Figure, 9
— Bach's use of, 31, 66–7, 104
— as used in development, 49–50
— as used in variations, 78–80
Figured bass, 17, 28
First-movement form, 8, 35
    in a concerto, 71
    abbreviation of, 35, *and cf.* 84
Folk-song, melodic organization of, 3–8
Free Fantasia, 40, *and see* Development
Fugue:
    early types of, 87–94
    as developed by J. S. Bach, 94–109
    accompanied, 111–12
    double, 110–11
    on a chorale, 112–14

Galliard, 22
Gavotte, 21
Ground, ground bass, 65, 81, 82

Hornpipe, 22

Impromptu, viii
Introduction, to a sonata, 33 (*note*)
— to an overture, 82, 83

Inversion, harmonic, *see* Double Counterpoint
— melodic, 47, 106–7

Jig, 20

Key-System:
in a concerto exposition, 71
in first-movement form, 40–4, 51, 52
in fugue, 96–102
in rondo form, 61
in sonatas of the Bach type, 29–30
in a suite, 23

Leit-motif, 125 (*note*)
Lessóns, 17 (*note*)
Lied form, 126
Loure, 21

Madrigal, 16, 127
Mass, 74, 126
Minuet, 20, 33–4
Modal system, 4–5, 17, 87–9
Modulation, in the 16th century, 89–90
Motet, 16, 127
Musette, 21

Nocturne, viii

One-figure forms, 80
Ordres, 17 (*note*)
Overture, earlier form of, 82–3
— later form of, 84

Partita, 17 (*note*)
Passacaglia, 81–2
Passepied, 21
Pavan, 22
Period, 10
Phrase, balance of, in melody, 5–6
— definition of, 10
Plagal modes, 88–9, 100
Polonaise, 21
Prelude, viii, *and see* Chorale prelude

Quartet, String, 28–9, 32
Quodlibet, 76

Real answer, 92, 98
Recapitulation:
in first-movement form, 52–4, 56
in fugue, 96
as an essential element in ternary form generally, 8, 24
Redundant entries, 91, 102
Related keys, 30
Rhapsody, viii
Rhythm, alteration of:
as a method of thematic development, 47–9
in variation form, 74, 77
Rhythm, in the 16th century, 90–1
Rigadoon, Rigaudon, 21
Ritornello, 64, 65, 126
Rondo, shorter form of, 58–60
— longer form of, 60–2
— *see also* Sonata rondo
Round, 116–18

Saraband, 19–20
Scherzo, 33–4
Sentence, 10
Serenade, 25
Slow movement:
Bach type, 31, 65–6
Beethoven type, 35–7
Sonata, general definition of, 27
— classification into Bach and Beethoven types, 28
— Bach type, described, 28–32
— Beethoven type, described, 32–4
— *See also* First-movement form; Rondo; Scherzo; Slow movement
Sonata di Ballo, 18
— da Camera, 18–19, 28
— da Chiesa, 28
Sonata rondo, 58
Song form, 126
Stretto, 105–7
Subjects, fugal, classification of, 98
— 'Principal' and 'Second' (so-called), 41, 44
Suite, description of the movements in a, 18–22
— in modern times, 25
.Symphonic poem, 127
Symphony, 32

Ternary form, 8, 24
Tonal answer, 98–102
Transition section, 41
Trio, 28
— of a minuet, 20
— of a scherzo, 33–4
Tutti, 63–73 (*passim*)

Unit, 9

Variation form, 74–82
— in a slow movement, 37. *See also* Ground, Passacaglia, Chaconne

Working-out, *see* Development